CREATING CUSTOMERS

How to Increase Sales through Non-technique Selling

PAT WEYMES

KoganPage

London Philadelphia New Delhi

Publisher's Note

Indian Edition 2010

Kogan Page India Private Limited
4737/23 Ansari Road,
Daryaganj
New Delhi 110 002

This edition is for sale in the Indian subcontinent only. Not for export elsewhere.

ISBN : 978-81-7554-589-2

Published by Vinod Vasishtha for Kogan Page India Private Limited,
4737/23, Ansari Road, Daryaganj, New Delhi 110 002.

Printed and bound in India.

Contents

Introduction

Welcome to what I hope will prove to be one of the better investments you have made in furthering your selling career. To reinforce the wisdom of that investment, I can personally assure you that by applying the skills as outlined in this book, you will not only increase sales but also get a lot more fun out of your job. You will find the skills easy to apply, regardless of your current level of selling experience. The skills you will be exposed to are not just my personal experiences, they are the culmination of a lifetimes experience and study, supported by thousands of salespeople and endorsed by buyers from all parts of the globe.

WHAT I HOPE THIS BOOK WILL DO FOR YOU

Whatever your reasons for reading this book, I can promise that it will help you to:

- increase motivation, personal confidence and encourage better selling habits
- manage inter-personal relationships at work and in your personal life
- gain more enthusiastic support from managers, colleagues and friends
- maximize the use of your time and other precious selling resources
- gain a significant competitive edge at all stages of the selling process

- create winning proposals that will distinguish your ideas from the rest
- sell your products at a profit while simultaneously increasing buyer satisfaction
- significantly improve relationships with your present customers.

It will not come as any great surprise to hear that it just doesn't happen – you have got to make it happen. This means making an effort and carrying out all of the recommended steps. As a wise man once said: 'the only place where success comes before work is in the dictionary'.

THE CONCEPT OF NON-TECHNIQUE SELLING

Thousands of salespeople have tried and tested the principles outlined in this book. Not only do they vouch for the effectiveness of these skills, but they have also claimed dramatic increases in sales by putting them into practice. Even for the most experienced of salespeople, it only required a small but significant shift in attitude and approach. Whether you are just starting your career or have been selling for years, I do promise that you will increase your sales – provided that you follow all the recommendations.

Like many experienced salespeople, I too have been indoctrinated in the need to develop techniques in order to maintain a competitive edge. Even today, sales consultants all over the world make a good living convincing trainees of the importance of developing these essential skills. Where I differ from my fellow sales training professionals is my unshakeable belief that sales techniques are outdated and no longer applicable.

Throughout my extensive selling career I have never felt comfortable with the suggestion that techniques or programmed responses are required to elicit a sale from a customer. This is not to imply that all sales training is only about techniques – it most certainly is not. In fact, many of the more positive skills I learned on my first sales course, I still use today and you will read many of them later.

I have tried to argue the case in favour of non-technique selling by giving common sense examples and emphasizing the importance of looking at techniques from the buyer's viewpoint. If you are not entirely swayed by what I have written, I propose that you talk to as many buyers as possible to get them to confirm that this is a more acceptable selling approach.

As we will discuss, there is a difference between persistence and persecution. There is a gulf in the attitudinal approach between salespeople who look for customers and those who look for sales. Most important of all, we exaggerate our need to develop techniques when the evidence clearly states that their influence in the sale is minimal. I will go as far as to say that in some cases the use of a technique could actually cost you a sale.

If you have been selling for many years and you find yourself constantly asking for the order and not getting it or hearing too many buyers say:

'Lets skip the spiel and get down to business'

'I need more time to think about this'

`You are much too expensive'

'Leave your card and I will get back to you'

I believe you are doing something very wrong indeed. By the time you have finished reading this book I hope that you too will enthusiastically endorse this important concept.

THE NEED TO INVEST YOUR TIME

Because selling enters into every form of human activity, it's really more akin to a science than just a series of skills. Yet the overwhelming majority of salespeople invest only a few hours per year developing their skills. Theoretically, a salesperson that has five years' experience should be considerably better than when he started selling. Somebody taking up golf or any other sport would expect to see a definite improvement each year. However, salespeople who have sold for 20 years and have never attended training sessions do not necessarily have 20 years' experience. They frequently have one year's multiplied by 20, and there is a difference.

KEEPING AHEAD OF THE 'POSSE'

There are 8760 hours in a year, but few salespeople spend even 87 hours (1 per cent) of their year trying to improve their understanding of selling. Yet the constant development of our selling skills is essential. Here are a few very good reasons for improving your selling knowledge.

- There is no such thing as a 'born salesperson'. While the gift of a natural, pleasing, inoffensive personality is an advantage, it is never enough to guarantee consistently good selling results.
- Only informed people get results. Customers do not expect you to know everything but they do expect you to be knowledgeable, up to date and precise.
- The same selling situation will rarely reoccur and there is no such thing as a 'standard' sale. Customers will rightly expect you to adjust your thinking to their particular circumstances.

Different customers have different motives. Ten buyers may buy the same product for ten very different reasons and the salesperson has to uncover their individual needs. The marketplace is always changing. No organization can afford to stand still; as more is demanded of your customers more will be demanded of you.

Selling time is expensive. While sales targets are ever increasing, we will never have any more than 24 hours in a day. We need to be constantly seeking out new ways to improve selling efficiency without lowering customer satisfaction.

A salesperson competing against a rival of equal knowledge will have some chance, but a salesperson selling against a rival with superior knowledge has little chance indeed.

THE GESTALT THEORY

The Gestalt Theory, which is supported by scientific researchers, claims that the average person uses no more than 10 per cent of their mental capacity. If this is the case, the potential for personal development is enormous. Whatever you've achieved at this moment in life, you've done so operating on no more than 10 per cent of your resources.

HOW TO GET THE MOST OUT OF THIS BOOK

It's my sincere wish that you will get as much as you possibly can from this programme and I list here a few helpful ideas on how to maximize the benefits:

Keep an open mind

Keep an open mind on the material as you read it. Many of the ideas are so radical and so different from other sales books that it is easy to dismiss the ideas without due consideration. Please do not make judgements until you have finished the programme, particularly if you have previously undertaken a sales training course.

Talk to people who buy!

It is probably a good idea to bounce your ideas off people who are not directly involved in selling – at least for the moment. Talk to people who buy. Get their ideas and perceptions of selling and salespeople and see what you can learn from this research. Practically all of these ideas can also be applied to your social life, so practice the skills and demonstrate that they really do make a difference.

Try out the skills

Carry out all the required steps. Confidence can only come from knowledge and successful experience. Discovering that this approach works will feed your motivation.

Think of how the skills *do* apply

One of the biggest stumbling blocks to learning is the stubborn resistance to change old habits. Even a successful method may be improved upon. Especially try to avoid thinking, 'That would not work with my customers.' It's unwise to generalize – we deal with many different personalities, each with unique reasons for buying.

Enjoy the book and I hope that you will get a lot of positive ideas out of it!

1

The Concept of Non-technique Selling

Professional selling is a process, which if carried out correctly, will lead smoothly to customers giving you business. This chapter will help you to put selling into perspective, and it will also help you to build the attitudes and skills of a non-technique sales professional.

In this chapter we discuss:

- the difference between non-technique selling and other approaches to sales
- how selling is perceived by buyers and salespeople
- the essential skills of non-technique selling.

There are many ways to learn the skills of the successful salesperson:

- learning from personal experience – often referred to as the 'school of hard knocks'
- learning from the experience, the successes, and the failures of others
- having intensive training by the experts in the profession – the customer
- combining all the experiences – your own, others', and customers'.

The easiest way of acquiring skills and knowledge is having the facts from every source and using them to your advantage.

Significantly, the most important trainer of all – the customer – is rarely consulted on his or her views as to how we should approach them for the purpose of selling. This chapter is an attempt to redress that situation.

PUT YOURSELF IN THE BUYER'S SHOES

Of all the exercises that you will be asked to complete, this is the most important one. Your long-term attitudes towards selling could well be greatly influenced by the outcome – so please take your time!

Prioritize the skills

Please break the six selling skills which follow into two groups of three. Group one will include skills you consider to be the most important, and group two, the least important. Remember: YOU are the buyer:

1. Fluency of speech
2. Sales technique
3. Ability to listen
4. Interested in telling you about the (salesperson's) company
5. Interested in learning about your company
6. Integrity of the salesperson

Three selling situations

You are a senior buyer in a major international organization. Your role is to buy quality products at the best possible price. Your company's profits, and ultimately your own job prospects, depend largely on your ability to fulfil that function successfully. You deal with good, bad and mediocre salespeople every day, so you know how they operate.

The brief given by senior management is to purchase hi-tech security, estimated to cost US$250,000. You pick up the *Yellow Pages*, select the companies most capable of delivering and invite three salespeople to meet you. You know little or nothing about security equipment so you are at the mercy of the salespeople.

Selling situation 1

You have appointments with the three invited salespeople. Salesperson number one is well-dressed, mannerly and pleasant. After a brief introduction he proceeds to tell you:

- that his company is the largest
- they have the best products
- they have a huge customer base
- they have branches around the world

He then:

- shows you illustrations of major installations
- tells you about their superb after sales service
- hands you colourful, professionally produced brochures.

The call lasts about 12 minutes and you note that the salesperson talked for ten of those minutes. What impression have you formed of this salesperson? Did he strike you as:

- skilful and professional?
- typical of salespeople?
- a great salesperson?
- a very poor salesperson?

Selling situation 2

Salesperson number two gives a very good account of herself, but you notice that she is using expressions such as:

- 'When we install the equipment…
- 'Will I invoice you or the head office?'
- 'Do you want me to arrange the training or will you do it yourself?'

At this stage you are still researching the options available to you. Would you:

- be persuaded to do business?
- be persuaded not to do business?
- perceive her approach as arrogant?
- take a mental note without reacting?
- ask her to leave?

Selling situation 3

Salesperson number three arrives. After fairly extensive discussion you tell the salesperson that you need time to consider and that you will call him. The conversation goes as follows:

Salesperson: 'Is there something that I haven't explained properly?'
You (the buyer): 'No; I am happy with what you have told me. I want to look at other proposals and then I will decide on the best option.'
Salesperson: 'From what you have seen, do you think it is along the lines of what you are looking for?'
You: 'It seems to cover all of our needs adequately.'
Salesperson: 'If you are happy with the product, and as you say it addresses your needs, is there anything else that would prevent you from going ahead with an order today?'
You: 'Well… it is a major purchase; I need to consider all the details and as I mentioned to you already, I have to look at other proposals.'
This exchange continues for another five minutes.
Salesperson: 'What do I have to do to get you to give me the business today?'
You: 'I am not going to give you the business today. You will have to excuse me, but I must attend another meeting.'
Salesperson's last throw of the dice: 'If I include a monitor for your own office as part of the package at no additional charge – can we do business?'
You: 'Interesting offer, but not today thank you – look, I really must go!'

Salesperson: 'You know of course that you won't get a better deal from anybody else?'
You now reflect on the sales call. Based on the exchange that has taken place between you, please consider the following:

- rate his chances of getting the business today:
- extremely good
- extremely poor
- no opinion
- absolute zero

Would his persistence in closing:

- influence you to buy?
- influence you not to buy?
- buy only if you have to?
- not influence you at all?

Going over your responses

In the first exercise I asked you to list in order of priority six selling skills. According to buyers, this is the way they should have been listed.
Most important:

- integrity of the salesperson
- interest in learning about your company
- ability to listen.

Least important:

- fluency of speech
- interested in telling you about his company
- sales technique.

How you placed them in each group is unimportant. What is essential is that you put the right skills in each group.

What the exercise tells us is this: integrity, listening to, and showing interest in the buyer and his or her company is of far greater importance to the buyer than sales 'technique'.

I possess a library of books, sales manuals and videos on selling and each one highlights the need for sales 'technique' to give a competitive edge. Yet the target of all our efforts – the buyers – are telling us that 'techniques' are less important than integrity, listening skills and fact-finding. Is there a book anywhere in the world entitled *Integrity: the Key to Successful Selling?*

Selling situation 1

In the first selling situation, the salesperson spends all your time 'selling' his company, his product, his service. No attempt was made to uncover your needs or to give you time to ask questions or explain your problem – before he started selling. For a combination of these reasons you would have been correct in rating him as a very poor salesperson.

In fairness to salespeople, when this serious error is pointed out to them, they can see immediately where and why they lose sales. The question is, why were they selling like that in the first place?

Selling situation 2

In the second selling example, this woman, well tutored in sales techniques, realizes the value of 'assumptive selling' (keep assuming that you have got the sale and when you meet with no resistance the sale is yours!). Each question is deliberately worded to force a commitment from the buyer. This may take in a number of customers. A number may be amused. Some will show the salesperson the door. Some will be very angry.

Most people find this technique infuriating; the probable answer was that you would have been 'persuaded not to buy'.

Selling situation 3

In the final example, the salesperson continues in his attempt to close the sale. There is a very narrow line between persistence and persecution: persistence in asking twice for the business may be admired, but asking more than twice is likely to be perceived as persecution. His chances of getting the business today? Absolute zero (you made that clear at the start). Most buyers claim that his performance would influence them not to buy!

The ABC of selling is: 'always be closing'; sales courses and books extol the virtues of constantly asking for the order! Yet buyers consistently say such a badgering approach is a sales turn-off.

I accept that you may never have been sold to in this manner and for that reason these examples might look extreme. However, I suggest that you talk to buyers who deal a lot with salespeople and they will tell you how frequently they are exposed to these types of selling approaches.

The purpose of putting the exercise to you was to:

- highlight the need to see the selling process from the customer's point of view – a strongly marked weakness in salespeople universally
- put into perspective the grossly overstated value of the need for sales 'techniques'
- demonstrate that, contrary to increasing orders, the use of sales techniques could actually cost you sales.

FROM THE DINOSAUR DAYS OF SELLING TO THE PRESENT DAY

The early pioneers of sales training used a mnemonic AIDA to refer to what they called the 'steps of the sale'. This stands for Attention, Interest, Desire and Action. This method of selling was based on four main principles:

- attention – strong handshake and confident introduction
- interest – a big interest-getting statement such as: 'What would you say if I could increase your sales by 50 per cent?'
- desire – this involved testimonials from other happy buyers with a strong subliminal suggestion 'this could be you!'

- action – the all-important close where you persist in asking for the order until you get the sale.

I believe that this system is past its sell-by date and totally inconsistent with the creed of non-technique selling. Some of these principles still apply but professional selling has evolved and today's buyer expects the process to be more interactive. Compare that system with the following one and decide which is the most professional.

Pre-call preparation; approach to the buyer; establishing rapport; fact-finding the customer's specific needs; setting up another appointment; studying the best options that you can offer; matching your product with customer's requirements; submitting a proposal or quotation; discussing and satisfying the customer's concerns; completing all the necessary documentation; ensuring the product is delivered as agreed; and finally, keeping in touch with the customer.

If you can sincerely adopt this method of selling, I promise that you stand out from so many other salespeople who try to take costly short cuts. If you try this method and it does not make a significant difference to the selling atmosphere, please write to me, I will be interested to find out why it is not working for you.

Pressure selling doesn't work!

Sales success comes from being able to climb inside the customer's head. Most customers will never tell a salesperson outright why their sales pitch is a failure. Instead, they'll use dismissive phrases such as: 'I am too busy at the moment', 'We are happy with our present supplier', 'Your product is too expensive.'

These may be genuine objections, but often hide the customer's real objections: 'I do not like you or your manner; please leave and don't come back.' The salesperson is left to guess what went wrong.

Consider how many times you've gone into a shop and felt under pressure to buy, or have been so annoyed at the standard of service that you have walked out. Few people voice disapproval to the offending salesperson. The people you call on are no different.

REINFORCING THE MYTHS ABOUT SALES TECHNIQUES

When you consider that salespeople are among the highest-paid earners, it is disappointing that some old, unfair perceptions remain. The day is rapidly approaching when salespeople will have be graduates, or at the very least, possess some measurable qualification before being offered a selling role. If a company employs 100 salespeople and they are all selling their own way, then they can not all be selling the right way. Until such times as standards exist, perceptions will always be at the mercy of the people who represent the profession.

'Always be closing?'

The number of books written on this one aspect of selling would fill any library. As a person who has spent his entire life in this profession, I firmly believe that all salespeople would benefit more from books written on how to 'open' the sale.

I will not waste your valuable time providing techniques and skills that you will never need. I would rather assure you that asking for the business is the least complicated part of the selling process. I can not subscribe to the most over-rated technique of all —'keep asking for the order' – and it is important to say that in my own personal experience, whenever a customer had decided against my proposal, and then subsequently changed his mind – it was never because I had used a technique.

Buyers who have genuine problems are looking for solutions. If you cannot solve the problem, no technique will get you the sale. If you can offer a solution, why would the buyer act like a moron and wait until you have asked ten times before giving you the order?

'Never give up?'

Some people can do more damage to the sales profession in the space of a few minutes then others could do in a lifetime. By way of illustration, during the time that I was writing this book, I watched a documentary on selling shown on Channel Four. It outlined the difficulties of hundreds of salespeople selling a domestic product. Anyone who cared about the selling profession would be extremely disappointed with the message it conveyed.

The programme outlined a sales training session, and included inspiring guidance such as: 'In selling – you never give up asking for the order.' This is contrary to what I believe. Another piece of wisdom offered: 'People will mirror whatever you do, so keep agreeing with customers and they will have to agree with you.' (Really?)

When programmes like this are produced, it is not surprising that public perceptions of salespeople are so poor. This film could have been made in one of thousands of highly professional sales operations yet the film-makers choose one of the very few that reinforces people's beliefs that selling is a dreadful job!

Unsurprisingly, many of the very fine people who joined this particular company stayed only a short time there and based on their subsequent interviews, will not be looking for other jobs in selling. The company projected itself as a cross between a brainwashing organization and a religious order, and by their own admission, 'If you don't make it you have to go!' (in other words, if at first you don't succeed – you're fired!).

As a professional salesperson, two issues concern me about this film:

1. The people who didn't make the grade were trained in what they thought were 'selling skills' and are lost forever to selling.
2. This company put hundreds of people through their course and only a minority survived more than three months. Many of these people made no money at all. What are they going to tell the world about selling?

The programme reinforced the cynical view that in order to be successful in selling, three special attributes are needed: a hard neck (presumably to take abuse and insults); the capacity to develop and deliver a sales 'spiel'; and the ability to convince people to buy things they don't really need.

If this really is what selling is all about, I will change my career in the morning. Fortunately, the reality is different.

SALESPEOPLE'S PERCEPTIONS OF SELLING

Even salespeople sometimes don't think too highly of their profession. Why do salespeople camouflage their selling roles by using titles such as: 'Account Executive', 'Marketing Consultant', or 'Area Manager'. It is alright to use such professional-sounding titles provided you are not trying to deceive the customer, or (more disappointingly) because you don't want people to think you are only a salesperson. Never forget, we are not just another spoke in the wheel of economic progress – we are the wheel.

We should always remember that when we call on customers, we represent not only ourselves and our organizations but also our profession. People outside of selling will never think more highly of the profession than the people who represent it!

BUYERS' PERCEPTIONS OF SELLING

I have no way of knowing how you responded to the earlier exercises on selling situations, although I hope that you agree with those provided by buyers. Their answers are consistent with the principles of non-technique selling:

- 'techniques' are the ultimate turn-off
- 'skills' are positive – 'techniques' are negative!
- 'if you're only interested in a sale – forget it!'
- 'don't sell to me – just help me to buy'.

Let us look at these points one by one.

'Techniques' are the ultimate turn-off

Salespeople learn sales techniques because it has always been assumed that they are an integral part of the selling role. On the other hand, buyers perceive the blatant use of jaded 'techniques' as an insult to their intelligence. They hear these techniques so frequently they can actually identify the 'boomerang method', the 'sharp angle close' and the 'if' technique. Forgive me if I don't explain them here, you won't be needing them!

If the ability to build mutual trust is the key to successful selling, how can this be achieved if the customer thinks that you are using sneaky, underhanded methods to get a sale?

Remarkably, no-one appears to have undertaken research to discover if these 'techniques' actually increase sales, or to measure salespeople's performance on the basis of 'before and after'. If techniques were viewed in a positive light by buyers, we would never hear them say: 'Let's skip the spiel and get down to business', and 'Forget about the "sales talk", just tell me what it does.'

Recently, in a consultancy capacity, I accompanied a salesperson on a sales visit. Having given a reasonable account of himself, he then went for the 'close'. The buyer thought for a moment and responded politely with: 'I am sorry but on this occasion my answer will have to be no.' The salesperson, doctrinated in the belief that when the customer says no, he is really only looking for more information, rejoined: 'You obviously have a reason for saying no – may I ask you what you mean?'The customer sat up, looked the salesperson in the eye, and said: 'I would be delighted to explain it to you, now tell me, what part of NO do you not understand?'

Subsequently, I got to know this customer and asked him about this incident (of which he had only a vague recollection). He told me: 'I meet at least 20 salespeople every week and it always infuriates me when these people think that by persecuting me for the business that I will change my mind. I must admit, when I hear a familiar technique I tend to overreact and that is probably what happened in that situation. When will salespeople ever learn that unless they can solve my problems, no magic words will alter my decision.'

'Skills' are positive – 'techniques' are negative

Buyers are extremely impressed with what they discern as skilful selling! In their view, professional selling is 'something that is happening up front where we can see the salesperson's skills in action!' These skills could be a combination of admirable attributes such as: skilful questioning and genuine interest in helping the customer; overall integrity of the presentation; knowledge of the market, the product and competitive activity; enthusiasm for the job and company; and personal appearance.

How did you rate sales techniques in Selling Situation 1? (p 12). If you placed them in group two, then you also agree with the buyers!

'If you are only interested in a sale – forget it'!

Too many sellers are only interested in the bottom line – to get a sale. Their selling strategy is based on brief short-term relationships and once their business is concluded, they turn their attention to the next prospect. Putting it in very brutal terms, the sales plan is 'get in, get a sale and get out'! Salespeople who look for sales tend to:

- think short-term (where will I get this month's targets?)
- separate the market into prospects (people who might buy now) and suspects (people who probably won't buy now)
- try to close the sale on every call (even though the buyer is not ready to buy)
- have lots of 'call backs'
- usually have poor selling hit rates (ratio of calls to sales).

Salespeople who only look for sales get this consistent objection from customers: 'I want to think it over.' If you hear this a lot, it is time to look at your sales approach. The later session on fact-finding skills may be of special interest.

'Don't sell to me – just help me to buy'

The sales trainer's cry of 'keep asking for the order' sits very uncomfortably with the old axiom 'a man convinced against his will is of the same opinion still'. Both of these statements cannot be right!

The popular sales training creeds of: 'See a lot of customers and ask them all to buy', 'Remember the ABC of selling – always be closing', and 'Persistence is the key to success – keep asking for the order', are diametrically opposed to everything that professional selling should be about. If your business is one where orders or products can be repeated or upgraded, you will not enhance your relationship by persecuting the buyer for the order when common sense would suggest that the customer is not ready to buy! For example, you walk into a department store to buy some new clothes. The moment you walk in a salesperson comes over and inquires: 'Can I help you?' Like most people, you respond, ' No thank you, I am just looking around.' You start looking through a rack of clothes and you feel the sales assistant's hot breath on the back of your neck, and she says: 'Was there something in particular you were looking for?' You reply: 'No, nothing in particular', as you investigate the quality of a garment. Again the salesperson asks: 'Would you like to try it on?' Every day, millions of people all over the world are exposed to this level of pressure to buy. The majority protest with their feet and walk out! The moral: there is absolutely no point in pressurizing people when they are not ready to buy.

THE PRINCIPLES OF NON-TECHNIQUE SELLING

Apart from my views and others' experiences on the merits of practising non-technique selling, here are a few other persuasive reasons:

- contrary to entrenched sales training messages, there is absolutely no evidence that techniques have any positive influence on today's buyer or the outcome of the sale
- we do know that most senior buyers are not impressed with the use of techniques and in some cases they could actually encourage them not to buy
- given the choice, buyers would prefer that salespeople were 'up front' in all their dealings
- while sales techniques may score highly in the classroom, they are of least importance at the sales interview.

Here I can speak with authority: salespeople who dispense with techniques and practice the skills outlined in this course claim a noticeable and frequently a dramatic turnaround in sales. If you need further proof of the role techniques play in selling, ask a friendly buyer to confirm or deny the points listed above. If you receive information to the contrary, I hope you will write to me.

This concept has five major principles, and are the foundation on which non-technique selling skills are based. They are:

- think, act and communicate on the basis of win/win!
- customers like to think that you care
- look for customers – not sales
- people buy people first
- in order to increase sales – you must stop selling!

Whenever I outline this philosophy to experienced salespeople, it is greeted with derision. But I give you my assurance, every salesperson who has ever been exposed to these skills has endorsed this set of values with enthusiasm – and I believe you will too. So let's briefly take these principles one by one.

Think, act and communicate on the basis of win/win!

We will talk about win/win in Chapter 3 but a brief reference at this stage is in order. People who practice the philosophy of win/win communication will help to create a cooperative rather than a competitive selling environment.

I hope that as you progress through the book that everything you read, and all suggestions made, will be on the basis of both parties winning – you and your customers! Techniques are contrary to the spirit of win/win communication, and salespeople who persist in their use will leave countless orders behind them.

Customers like to think you care

The best way to win customers is to demonstrate that you really do care about them. The sales manager of one of the most successful companies I am associated with has a very simple selling maxim that he regularly tells his sales team: 'Go out and make friends with our customers.'

If, through words and deeds you can convince customers that you really do care about their businesses and their problems, you will be successful in any market conditions. Here are a few questions to stimulate some action.

- Does your company have a corporate customer service philosophy? By this I mean a set of agreed standards, accepted, endorsed and practised by everybody, not just a chosen few?
- How do your customers register their views on the service you and your company provide?
- How often will the customer receive visits from you or your company without a sale being the ultimate objective?

- What do you do to convince customers that you appreciate their business?
- Do you have a personal customer care philosophy that you practice, every day, week, month or year?

If you answer yes to these questions, you are part of a tiny minority, congratulations! If you answer in the negative, is it time for some new thinking?

Look for customers – not sales

There is a major attitudinal difference between salespeople who look for sales and those who look for customers. Salespeople who look for customers have an entirely different approach. They recognize that there are many steps to creating customers, and their first call is just for the purpose of establishing rapport and fact-finding. Salespeople who look for customers:

- recognize the importance of building relationships
- are more relaxed in the initial approach (they are not trying to 'sell' on this call)
- realize the importance of proper fact-finding
- get more valuable information – as there is less pressure
- create an impression because they do something different (others are trying to get a sale)
- have plenty of time to consider creative response (are not under pressure to produce solutions on the spot)
- hit rates tend to be extremely high (less calls and more quality sales).

As we progress through this book the points made here will become very clear. What is essential is that you believe in the approach of looking for customers and not sales!

People buy people first!

We know from research that buying decisions are up to 84 per cent emotional. In other words, if the customer feels that he or she does not want to buy from you – it's fairly certain that you won't get the business. Decisions are personal and the relationship with the buyer is critical. Yet professional salespeople score poorly on: creating a positive first impression; fact finding skills; taking a genuine interest in customers' needs; creating personalized proposals and quotations; proactive customer care; reactive customer service; human relations skills; communication skills; and personal confidence

Significantly, salespeople think they score highly in these skills, but the reality is different. By the end of this book, you will have been exposed to crucial skills that your rivals may never have taken time out to develop.

If you want to increase sales – stop selling!

An excellent definition of non-technique selling is 'helping people to make up their minds'. The best way to achieve this is by:

- uncovering precisely what it is that customers are trying to achieve
- being personally convinced that your product or service is a solution
- explaining precisely how your product addresses your customers' needs
- offering reassurance when they express concerns
- providing supporting information to assist them in making the purchase.

Compare this to one of the cardinal mistakes even experienced salespeople are inclined to make – they start 'selling' the product or service without the most basic fact-finding information. In many cases, buyers' needs are only of secondary consideration and in these circumstances, selling is extremely difficult! 'Selling' is something that happens at the later stages of the interview and never at the start. If you want to increase sales dramatically, remember, the last thing you do is sell.

Throughout the remaining chapters of this book we will return repeatedly to Non-technique selling, where the focus will be on creating and maintaining a win/win situation for you and your customer.

TEN KEY POINTS ON THE CONCEPT OF NON-TECHNIQUE SELLING

- If mutual trust is key to successful selling – where does that leave techniques?
- Salespeople see the need for techniques as an integral part of the job.
- There is factual evidence supporting the view that techniques increase sales.
- There is evidence that the use of 'techniques' offends many major buyers.
- We have to start seeing techniques from the customer's point of view.
- There is a major difference in looking for sales and looking for customers.
- Think, act and communicate on the basis of win/win.
- Customers resent being sold – start helping them to buy.
- If you want to increase sales, the last thing you should do is sell.
- Salespeople who dispense with techniques claim a highly positive response.

2

Confidence and Self-image

Let us now concentrate on the personal attributes critical to consistently returning a top sales performance:

- confidence
- self-image
- attitude
- motivation.

Not only are these attributes fundamental to selling, all four elements are so strongly intermingled, that they are interdependent: take away any one element from three and you are left with none!

In this chapter we will discuss how to

- capitalize on your strengths
- deal positively with setbacks
- set goals and retain the motivation to achieve them
- recognize and develop the personality traits that will help you sell.

Before exploring these areas let's do a little soul searching and please consider these questions as honestly as you can:

- What major achievements have you had in the past year?
- What promises did you make to yourself that you failed to act on?
- What promotions have you had in the past two years?
- What real improvements have you made in your living standards?

- What are you doing today that you were doing two years ago?
- What do you expect to be doing in five years?
- How many friends or colleagues have overtaken you on the road to success?
- Have you written goals for what you really want out of life?
- Are you presently realizing your full potential? And if not...
- When are you finally going to do something about it?

These questions are merely to provide the motivation to stop procrastinating and start doing! Most personal motivational problems have their roots embedded in some inability to overcome entrenched habits. It is very simple: change your habits and you will automatically change your attitudes – change your attitudes and you will automatically change your habits!

CAPITALIZE ON YOUR STRENGTHS

Confidence comes from the belief in our ability to do certain things. The only way we can develop that belief is through activity, through doing more things. This inevitably means taking risks, facing fear, and experiencing failure. The lessons learnt from failure help to build confidence. A baby taking its first steps will wobble and fall many times but in its determination to walk will dismiss completely all the failed attempts.

As Gerhard Gechwandtner wrote: 'Self-doubt is nothing but a cover-up of our innate strengths, over confidence is nothing but a cover-up of our weaknesses.'

Confucius said that failure is not falling down, it is falling down and refusing to get back up again. Remember that it is all right to forget your mistakes, provided you learn from their lessons.

WANT TO BE THE BEST

At some stage in your career you have got to make a decision, do you want to be mediocre or do you want to be the very best? It will always be easy to be mediocre but if you are going to be the best it is really going to hurt.

As in all professions, salespeople generally fall into one of three categories: poor, mediocre and outstanding: 10 per cent are very poor at what they do; 80 per cent are in the mediocre to good category; and 10 per cent are outstanding – because they do something different.

Make the decision right now to do whatever is necessary to be in this top 10 per cent. While all the suggested steps may look daunting, remember that a journey of a thousand miles starts with the very first step.

PRACTISE WHAT YOU CAN'T DO!

Good salespeople have to develop a multitude of talents and it is the exceptional person who comes to the profession with all the skills intact. If what you believe to be a weakness is holding you back, start working on it now! Instead of saying: I am fearful of making presentations to groups; I am intimidated by senior buyers; I am a poor letter writer; I am not a very assertive person, start saying 'that's the way I used to be but today is a different story'.

To offer some personal reassurance, throughout my life, I have always had an innate fear of speaking in public, today I make my living from it!

Learn from experience

A common denominator of successful salespeople is that they are excellent students of their profession. They are the epitome of whom Chesterfield said:

> There are three classes of people in this world. The first learn from their own experience – these are the wise. The second learn from the experience of others – these are the happy. The third neither learn from their own nor the experiences of others – these are the fools.

Throughout this book we will attempt to combine all of the experiences, yours, mine, the customers' and countless salespeople who share their successes and failures. You don't have to re-invent the wheel, there is a less painful way to gain confidence.

YOUR OWN WORST ENEMY?

Did it ever cross your mind when looking in the bathroom mirror in the morning that you may be looking at your number one competitor? Your daily behaviour and general attitude could cost you dearly. Try to answer these questions honestly.

- Do you always listen to the news before you start work?
- Are you usually in good humour in the mornings ?
- Do you always speak well of others?
- Are you good-natured about a decision that goes against you?
- Do you try to see the positive points in people?
- Are you easily offended?
- Are you always punctual?

Let's be honest about this, listening to the news may put you in an alert and interested frame of mind but it may also dampen your good humour. There is also the added danger that you will use this 'bad news' as a way to break the ice with contacts. It may get them talking but it is unlikely to do anything for their motivation to buy! Keep a mental note of your answers as you read through the next couple of chapters.

Image and imagination

Our imagination plays a bigger part in our lives than most of us realize. Will-power is not the dominating factor in achieving our goals. When our imagination is in conflict with our will, imagination wins every time. For example, if you will yourself to be successful at something while at the same time imagining that you will fail, it is impossible to succeed. If, on the other hand, you can imagine yourself succeeding, you're half way there.

The power of imagination has been well documented in cases of hypnotism and autosuggestion. Many of us are 'hypnotized' into thinking that we are destined to be failures, so we behave appropriately. If you see yourself as a shy, unassertive, mediocre salesperson, your behaviour will tend to support your own concept of who you are. Meeting a customer thinking that you haven't got a chance of getting the business – in practically every case you will find that you were right.

When convinced that the hypnotist's words are true, a good hypnotic subject can do surprising things. The subject who is told that he is at the North Pole will not only shiver and appear to be cold but will also develop goose-bumps.

Emil Coue, the 19th century French physicist, was famous for his amazing cures through the method of autosuggestion. Remember the phrase 'every day in every way I am getting better and better' . He believed that the imagination was the key to self-cure. There is plenty of hard factual evidence to support his suggestions. Hospital beds all over the world are filled with people who have worried themselves into serious illness. People have died when they should have lived, while others have lived when they should have died.

Dr Maxwell Maltz has spent many years researching the subconscious power. His book *Psychocybernetics* is hailed as a classic of its genre and tells us that:

> The nervous system cannot tell the difference between an imagined and a real experience and the nervous system

reacts appropriately to what we imagine to be true. For example, if you ate spaghetti but subsequently thought you had eaten worms – you would probably become quite ill!

According to aeronautical engineers; there is absolutely no known way that the bumblebee can fly. It is physically impossible for such flimsy wings to maintain the bee's body weight in flight. The only conclusion they can come to is that nobody has told the bumblebee.

Remember that it is not what you think you are that holds you back, it's what you think you are not! If you think negatively the result will be negative, whereas if you think positively you will create an atmosphere which makes positive results almost a certainty. An unknown writer put it very well when he wrote:

If you think you are beaten, you are,
If you think you dare not, you don't,
If you'd like to win, but think you can't,
It's almost certain you won't.
Life's battles don't always go
To the stronger or faster man
But sooner or later
The man who wins
Is the man who thinks he can!

Breaking through false ceilings

The reasons why most of us rarely maximize our capabilities are due to the many influences that dictate our mental development. For example: how many times have you had your enthusiasm for an idea or project dampened by someone saying:

- Sounds much too good to be true.
- Take my word for it, it's not as simple as it seems.
- You may as well dream here as in bed.
- You will never be the man your father was.
- If it was that easy, how come someone else hasn't done it

before now?
- It's not what you know, it's who you know.

HOW TO DEAL POSITIVELY WITH SETBACKS

Eleanor Roosevelt once said, 'nobody can ever make you feel inferior without your consent'. In our selling role, when it comes to self-evaluation we tend to sell ourselves short. There is a very good chance that you are smarter and much more creative than you think you are.

Our self-image is a mixture of positive and negative traits but when confidence is low we tend to dwell only on the negative. As a special exercise, take as much time as necessary to write down all the positive qualities you possess. For example:

- I dress well and I look professional.
- I am good at interpersonal relationships.
- I have made a happy family life.
- I have lots of skills to offer my employers.
- I consider myself a top salesperson.
- I am open-minded and prepared to learn.

Write up a diary of all of your personal achievements and add to them regularly. Whenever you are feeling a little low or your confidence has taken a dive, take out the list and review the contents – it will give you the lift you need.

Prepare for take-off

Here are a few questions for you to ponder: if you didn't know how old you were what age do you think you would feel? How would you feel on Monday morning if you thought it was Saturday?

It has been said that a man flattened by an opponent will get up again but a man flattened by conformity stays down for good. Try to avoid measuring your success by what you have done compared with others, but compared with what you are capable of doing.

It will always be easy to follow the crowd but a crowd never progresses. The very first step towards leadership takes a man away from the crowd. People with positive attitudes have to put up with a certain amount of ridicule, but take consolation in the knowledge that no monument was ever erected in memory of a critic.

SEE PROBLEMS AS OPPORTUNITIES

One of the pillars of professional selling is the ability to remain optimistic. Walt Disney was said to have asked ten people for their views on a new idea and when all ten were unanimous in their rejection of it, he would work on it immediately.

Dale Carnegie, author of *How to Win Friends and Influence People* used to tell a true story of a New England man who inherited a farm in Florida. On his arrival, he discovered the farm was made up of sandy soil on which no crops would grow and if that wasn't enough, the place was also infested with rattlesnakes. Undeterred, he decided to become a rattlesnake farmer. He sold the skins for women's handbags and shoes and sold snake venom to hospitals for use as a serum. So many people heard of his achievements and wanted to visit that the town thrived as a tourist attraction.

The ultimate tribute came when the local townspeople decided to rename their town, Rattlesnake, Florida.

Beware the prophets of doom!

There will always be plenty of people to darken your day and it seems that they have been around for quite a while: Is this an accurate reflection of our times?

'Our earth is degenerate. Bribery and corruption are common. Children no longer obey their parents. The end of the world is evidently approaching.'

This quotation could have come from this morning's newspaper but it didn't. It was found carved on a stone slab in Assyria in 2800 BC. In the 1860s, the head of the US Patents Office wanted to close down because he believed that everything worthwhile had already been invented. The role of the professional salesperson is difficult enough without listening to soul-destroying comments. On a more positive note:

- Shy away from negative people – they will never pay your mortgage.
- When you have a negative thought, dilute it with plenty of positives.
- Have plenty of deals operating at once, never depend on the 'big kill'.
- Develop an unshakeable 'yes I can' mentality.

AVOID CONFUSING FACT WITH OPINION

In all my years of working with salespeople, I never cease to be amazed at the way so many really good people confuse facts with opinions. In practically every case it is the opinion that is most damaging. Frequently I hear: 'That company are obviously in trouble, because they have made several people redundant'; 'My month is ruined because I have had a major order cancelled.'

In the first case, it may be a fact that people have been made redundant but it is only an opinion that the company is in trouble. In the second case, it is a fact that a major order has been cancelled but it is only an opinion that the salesperson's month is ruined. Make sure that you are not a victim of your own negative opinions.

The need for enthusiasm

Dale Carnegie said the way to acquire enthusiasm is to believe in what you are doing and in yourself and to want to get something definite accomplished. Believe in: yourself and your ability to do the job; the integrity of your colleagues and your company; your product or service; the profession and industry that you represent.

The salesperson who really believes in each of these will automatically feel enthusiastic. Always keep one point uppermost in your mind: the prospective buyer will never think any more highly of you, your product, your company or your profession than you do.

SET YOUR OWN GOALS AND RETAIN THE MOTIVATION TO ACHIEVE THEM

We have two lives to lead: a personal and a business life and both require our attention. The amount of time invested in each can be compared to a weighing scales – devote too much time to one at the expense of the other and you will upset the balance.

Similarly, if you only develop the business side of your life and fail to work at human relations, you may make money but will you be happy? It is probably fair to say that in the history of mankind, there has never been a case of anybody on his or her deathbed saying 'I wish I had spent one more day in the office.'

Secret of motivation

Motivation literally means 'inspiration to action'. There are two types of motivation. External motivation operates through fear or incentive imposed by external influences such as, for example, a sales manager. This type of motivation is short-term and ceases once the need or fear has been satisfied or eliminated.

The second type of motivation, internal motivation, is the more powerful because it is long-term and alters inbred attitudes. It comes from developing a sincere desire for the things that you want most out of your job, your career and your life.

To aid your motivation it is vital to retain a sense of direction. A salesperson without a daily plan and daily targets is like a car without a steering wheel. Be crystal-clear about what you want and keep the benefits of your goals at the front of your mind all the time.

Setting goals

Any time I meet de-motivated salespeople, I only have to ask them where they expect to be in 12 months and the shrug of the shoulders tells me all I need to know. A goal-setting action plan involves:

- setting out realistic, achievable goals for every area of your life
- analysing the obstacles to overcome and actions required in achieving the goals
- setting target dates for the start and completion of each goal
- monitoring your progress
- giving yourself a reward for the attainment of your objectives.

It is part of our nature as human beings to strive towards some desirable goal. If we have nothing to aim for, we become bored and frustrated. Take charge of your life. Replace the frustration with some action planning and spend your time and energy in making your life better for you and your family. Remember, if you aim at nothing you will hit it every single time.

Stop putting things off

Procrastination has been called the thief of time and we all fall into its trap at some point or other. The first step to banishing this destructive trait forever is to recognize the futility of it and to be ruthless in its elimination. It leads to frustration, anxiety and a host of unsolved problems that generally only get worse.

As James Baldwin wrote: 'Not everything that is faced can be changed but nothing can be changed until it is faced.'

Many salespeople will put off writing quotations, making call backs or checking out customer queries with the result that orders, and tempers, are lost. This is merely habit. Resolve with determination to change.

The motivation to be gained from completing long overdue tasks can be considerable. To prove this point to yourself list three tasks that you have been putting off, set a short-term timetable for their completion and start now!

Keep also in mind that if you want to make an easy job seem hard, just keep putting off doing it.

GOAL-SETTING ACTION PLAN

Hints on completing your goal-setting action plan

- Your goals must be realistic. They should present a challenge but still be possible to attain. It is absolutely imperative that your goals are your own and are not unfairly influenced by others. It is, after all, your life, and sacrificing your desires for the sake of others will impact your motivation in a negative way.
- Next, you must really want whatever goals you decide on. Anything worthwhile usually involves hard work and goal-setting is no exception. You will need all your energy and motivation if things do not go according to plan. Developing the ability to picture vividly in your

mind what it is you want will help you to achieve the end result.

- Having decided on the goal, analyse exactly what you have to do to achieve it. Anticipate the obstacles that you will inevitably have to overcome and, of course, what you're going to do to solve them.
- There must be start and finish dates. A football match without a time limit would be pointless and there would be no winner.
- The rewards to you on achievement are extremely important. List them in as much detail as possible. They will feed your motivation and urge you on to success.

Your goals will obviously span different areas of your life – your career, your family life, and your development.

Writing down your goals helps to clarify your thinking and strengthens the commitment you are making with yourself. Fuzzy, misty thoughts will produce fuzzy, misty results. On the other hand, an organized plan will spur you into action and increase your determination to succeed. Allow your goals to be flexible. You will be a different person in five years' time and what you now think will make you happy may change. Take a few minutes to fill these in.

SETTING GOALS

There are five stages in Goal-Setting

1. **Itemize** (The master plan)
2. **Categorize** (Putting them into order)
3. **Prioritize** (Listing the priorities)
4. **Visualize** (Pictures to feed motivation)
5. **Realize** (Keeping a motivating record)

ITEMIZE

Write down all your goals, no matter how far fetched they may appear. Let your imagination run free.

CATEGORIZE

Separate your goals into the appropriate categories as listed here. List each goal in probable order of priority.

Personal goals (everything you ever wanted to achieve, etc)

Domestic and family goals (what the family would like to do together)

Educational goals (your further development)

Career goals (position you would like to achieve)

Repeat this exercise for every other area of personal importance, ie physical, recreational, material, spiritual and financial. Do not limit yourself to the number of goals and keep adding to it month after month and so on.

PRIORITIZE

List here the three, five, or ten things you have selected. Based on your own priorities.

VISUALIZE

Aids to visualization

Pictures, photographs, and other symbols to help me visualize my goals.

As an aid to visualizing the rewards you will receive when you reach your goal, the above space is provided for you to include picture, photographs, or anything else that helps you symbolize the goal you have set for yourself. Visualization helps sustain motivation and further aids you in making your goal a reality.

REALIZE (goals achieved)

As you achieve your goals list them here. This will help to reinforce your confidence and motivation in setting others.

Goal achieved completion date .... /.... /....
What it meant to me

Goal achieved completion date .... /.... /....
What it meant to me

Goal achieved completion date .... /.... /....
What it meant to me

Goal achieved completion date .... /.... /....
What it meant to me

GOAL-SETTING

Goals to be achieved

Action steps required to achieve

1	6
2	7
3	8
4	9
5	10

Obstacles or difficulties to be overcome

1
2
3
4
5
6
7
8
9
10

Rewards to me on achievement of goal

1	11
2	12
3	13
4	14
5	15
6	16
7	17
8	18
9	19
10	20

Start date: .... /.... /.... Finish date: .... /.... /....

I will monitor progress on the following dates

.... /.... /.... .... /.... /.... .... /.... /....

BE CREATIVE

Let us look at the qualities of the creative salesperson and ask yourself: Is this the impression I project to my customers, colleagues and associates?

- open to the views of other people
- inquisitive and wants to learn
- not discouraged by failure or negative comments from others
- prepared to make mistakes in an effort to learn
- prepared to persevere in the face of opposition or ridicule
- anxious to consider every possible angle
- believes that to every problem there is a solution
- multiplies ideas by seeking the ideas of others

Creativity can be learnt as a skill, provided that the person taking on the task is open to a new approach. Creativity is not something that we introduce to help plan our future, it is something we need to do in order to have a future!

SALES PERSONALITY

These are some of the traits required for a successful salesperson, forming the mnemonic PERSONAL SUCCESS SKILLS. Take a few minutes to fill in the sales personality development graph (see Figure 2.1) where you are asked to assess these traits in yourself:

- perseverance
- empathy
- resilience
- sincerity
- open mind
- neat appearance
- ambition to succeed

- loyalty
- self-confidence
- understanding of human relations
- common sense
- cooperation
- enthusiasm
- simplicity
- self-motivation
- sense of direction
- knowledge
- integrity
- listening ability
- leadership skills
- sense of humour

Sales personality definitions

The successful sales personality will have a combination of the qualities summed up in the phrase 'personal success skills'. When considering these qualities, bear in mind that every single one of them can be acquired.

Perseverance. The ability to continue on your course of action despite difficulties or opposition. In selling, the efforts expended today are rarely reflected in today's results. We may have to call many times before we finally reap the rewards. We must keep uppermost in our minds that in our profession the only alternative to perseverance is failure to sell.

Empathy. Probably the most important attribute in selling: the ability to put yourself mentally in the other person's shoes. It is the skill of experiencing the other person's feelings and emotions imaginatively. Many people confuse empathy with sympathy, yet there is a distinct difference. Sympathy literally means to 'be in favour of or agreement with one's mood of opinions', whereas empathy means to really understand, but not necessarily to agree.

Empathy only becomes possible if you can mentally see the selling process from the buyer's point of view. There is a

	0	1	2	3	4	5	6	7	8	9	10
Perseverance											
Empathy											
Resilience											
Sincerity											
Open mind											
Neat appearance											
Ambition to succeed											
Loyalty											
Self-confidence											
Understanding of human relations											
Common sense											
Cooperation											
Enthusiasm											
Simplicity											
Self motivation											
Sense of direction											
Knowledge											
Integrity											
Listening ability											
Leadership skills											
Sense of humour											
	0	1	2	3	4	5	6	7	8	9	10

Figure 2.1 *Personality development graph*

Spanish expression: 'In order to be a bullfighter you must first learn to be a bull.' In order to be a successful salesperson you must first learn to be a customer.

Resilience. The ability to bounce back from disappointment and recover strength quickly. In the role of a salesperson, there will be many times when you get that 'Maybe I'm not cut out to be a salesperson' feeling. Just about every professional has uttered those words at some time or another. We need resilience to remind us that we are members of one of the most exciting and most frustrating professions in the world, and that every day will bring new opportunities and many disappointments.

Thomas Edison suffered hundreds of failures before he finally invented the light bulb. In fact, many of the greatest inventions of our time would still be mere laboratory toys were it not for the resilience of their creators.

Sincerity. Being genuine and honest without conceit or pretence – one of those qualities that is rarely faked with any success. Your customer must know that you mean what you say, and that you pass on only correct information.

Open mind. An absence of prejudiced or narrow-minded views. It means allowing mental access to the opinions and views of others in an effort to learn from their experiences.

Neat appearance. If you claim to work for a successful company with superior products, then you must dress in a manner that is consistent with your company's image. You would be reluctant to buy goods that are badly wrapped out of concern for the contents. Similarly, the customer will be reluctant to buy from you if you are untidy or slovenly in appearance.

Ambition to succeed. The burning desire to achieve your predetermined objectives. Ambition must be coupled with an active determination to achieve your personal and business goals.

Loyalty. Being faithful to people you are under an obligation to defend or support. Customers find it refreshing to hear a salesperson speak well of his or her company and colleagues.

Self-confidence. Our belief in our own abilities. If you tell yourself subconsciously that you can't do something, you will find in every case that you were right. 'Skill and confidence', as an old proverb puts it, 'are an unconquered army.'

Understanding of human relations. The human touch – showing kindness and consideration to other people. In selling terms this means practising and developing a combination of various skills many of which will be discussed in the next section.

Common sense. The ability to absorb facts and learn from a new experience. All successful salespeople must be alert to opportunities to improve their performance. They aren't satisfied with today's results, they want to do better tomorrow. It also means being able to focus your strengths and efforts on the task in hand.

Cooperation. Working together with your colleagues, subordinates and superiors as a team trying to achieve one common goal. Putting aside petty differences of opinion for the sake of the company objectives. Working with your customers and making conscious efforts to offer a complete and flexible service.

Enthusiasm. The magic spark that gets support without ever having to ask for it. Not only is it contagious, it is also the greatest motivator known to man. It is the burning inner drive that helps us to persuade people without pressurizing them. It was Emerson who said that without enthusiasm nothing great was ever achieved.

Simplicity. Speaking a language that others understand. All the skills and sales techniques are useless unless you have the ability to communicate thoughts and ideas to others in a manner that is acceptable and easily understood.

Self-motivation. Internal motivation is more powerful than external motivation (eg fear of a boss) because it is long-term and alters inbred attitudes. It comes from developing a sincere desire for the things you want most out of life. As an example: it has often been said that you can bring a horse to the well but you can't make it drink; however, you will have no trouble getting it to drink if you begin by making it thirsty!

Sense of direction. Devise a daily plan and daily targets and keep the benefits of your goals at the front of your mind at all times.

Knowledge. Constantly searching for more information about the market-place and the trends of future months and years. Striving to perfect and update selling techniques, to improve sales presentations and to increase orders.

Integrity. Honourable standards of ethics and professionalism. Our profession operates to a set of accepted principles that must guide our conduct. By the very nature of our job we are exposed to temptations daily. Exercising a high standard of integrity will, at the very least, establish your credibility as a professional.

Listening ability. In the history of selling nobody ever listened themselves out of a sale. A winner listens, a loser just waits until it's his turn to talk. Joe Girard, the Detroit salesman who is credited in the *Guinness Book of Records* as 'the world's greatest salesman', put it in a nutshell when he said 'God gave us two ears and one tongue so we could listen more than we talk.' It was that philosophy that helped him sell 1425 individual new cars in one year.

Leadership skills. The ability to influence or direct your own course of action through your own efforts. We are either the masters or the victims of our destiny. Every salesperson has the option of being the passenger or the driver in his or her career.

Sense of humour. The ability to appreciate or express amusement. Selling is a very serious business but we need to have the ability to introduce humour and the common sense to use it where appropriate.

As a guide to your self-analysis seek the unbiased opinions of two others when completing the graph. What you may discover is that their view of you is quite different from the picture you have of yourself. Tot up your marks and appraise yourself against these scores.

201 to 220 – give up your job immediately and apply for sainthood

171 to 200 – an outstanding score – be sure it is realistic

141 to 170 – this figure suggests great personal confidence
111 to 140 – this is an excellent score and indicates great integrity.
81 to 110 – indicates the amount of work to be done. High on humility
00 to 80 – contact me – we need to talk!

Special exercises

Before you move on to the next chapter, it is essential that you carry out all of the recommended action steps. As a reminder they were:

- Set plenty of realistic goals – this is imperative.
- Write down all of the positive qualities that you believe you possess.
- Complete the personality development graph.
- From the rest of the material you have read, highlight all other areas that need to be addressed and make the decision to do it now!

TEN KEY POINTS ON CONFIDENCE AND SELF-IMAGE

- It is all right to forget your mistakes provided you learn from their lessons.
- Make the decision to be the very best at whatever you do!
- Practice what you cannot do. Think in terms of that's the way I used to be…
- Don't try to re-invent the wheel, capitalize on the experience of others.
- Use your imagination – see yourself as successful – not as a failure.
- Remember that nobody can make you feel inferior without your consent.

- Get into the habit of seeing the opportunities emerging from every problem.
- Associate with positive people – avoid the prophets of doom and gloom.
- Carry out a frequent mental overhaul – check what you think and say!
- Be creative – allow mental access to the ideas and views of other people.

3

Winning People's Support

In Chapter 2 we discussed the role that motivation plays in selling. In this chapter we will discuss:

- the essential skills of win/win communication
- the importance of developing outstanding interpersonal skills
- how to gain the enthusiastic support of customers, managers and friends.

THE ESSENTIAL SKILLS OF WIN/WIN COMMUNICATION

In order to win support, one of the first things we must do is to have a long, hard look at ourselves, so let's start with the important area of respect. We respect others because they possess admirable qualities and in the case of a salesperson these qualities might include:

- integrity – not tampering with the truth
- developing a reputation through providing outstanding service
- taking the initiative – coming up with new ideas before the competition
- understanding the product completely and customers nearly as well
- a readiness to straighten out complaints and misunderstandings

- ability to create new ideas to help – himself, his company and his customers
- genuine interest in the customer and his or her problems.

It is said that: 'You can make more friends in two months by becoming really interested in them than you can in two years trying to get them interested in you.'

How do you see yourself?

Ask yourself the following questions: Would I like to have me as a boss? Would I like to have me in the sales team? Would I like to have me as a spouse? Would I like to have me as a friend? Would I like to have me as a parent?

I have spent many years testing the validity of the material that you will be exposed to in this book and the skills apply to every aspect of life. Course delegates tell me that by treating a spouse, a colleague, a friend or a child in the same manner as we should a customer, our personal lives would be in great shape.

HUMAN RELATIONS AND WIN/WIN

In today's extremely competitive business world professional selling can never be comprehensive without a thorough understanding of the principles of win/win. Without constantly practising these skills, it is almost impossible to build a worthwhile relationship with colleagues, customers, friends or loved ones.

This crucial part of human interaction is an area so often taken for granted, yet salespeople who practice the following skills will have an enormous advantage over competitors – and achieve greater job satisfaction into the bargain.

THE IMPORTANCE OF THINKING WIN/WIN

If you really want to increase sales, win/win is the way to go! It is not a technique, it is a state of mind courted by the most mature of communicators. To fully appreciate the significance of win/win let us first look at more common but less favourable options:

- win/lose lose/win
- lose/lose
- win
- win/win or no sale

Win/lose lose/win

I have put these two headings together because I believe that they are inextricably linked. People who follow the creed of win/lose will themselves become victims of the reverse: lose/win. One example is the insensitive account clerk who writes to a slow–paying customer: 'Unless we hear from you within the next seven days we will be forced to take legal action against you' (we win/ you lose).

The customer pays the bill and the next time the salesperson calls, the customer says: 'We are buying from another supplier' (you lose/I win).

Let us take a few other examples. Frequently I come across people who, for various reasons, have experienced poor service from a supplier. Their motivation is fuelled by anger and a desire to make the offender suffer, and in writing to complain, may say things such as: 'I cannot believe you could possibly employ such stupid people'; 'I am writing to tell you how I feel about your dreadful service'; 'Your staff have caused me enormous embarrassment', and so on.

These letters may end with the threat of taking business elsewhere, demands for compensation, and finishing off with insulting remarks.

There is another group of people who quite deliberately use their position and power to achieve their own goals. Because they are so steeped in self–protection they approach negotiation with a predetermined motivation to secure their own interests at others' expense.

The win/lose mentality is the root cause of most motivational problems. It destroys relationships, encourages reprisals, discourages teamwork and eventually breaks the spirit of the most enterprising people. It has no place in selling.

The Chinese have a saying: 'If a man sows beans he will reap beans.' In selling if we sow aggression we will reap aggression.

Lose/lose

Lose/lose is a belief in total destruction. Whenever two stubborn, egotistical individuals interact with one other, there can be only one result: lose/lose. Their sole motivation is fuelled by revenge or a desire to 'get even'. In spite of the fact that they know they are also going to lose, the desire to ensure that the other person suffers is greater than the pain of their own loss.

In one highly acrimonious divorce case recently, the judge ordered a man to split all the family assets down the middle with his wife. As a believer in 'getting even' his first stop on the way home was to the local hardware store to hire a chain saw. We can only guess at the perverted pleasure he experienced as he systematically cut his way through every piece of furniture they possessed. This grave piece of wisdom says it all:

> Here lies the body of William Jay
> Who died maintaining his right of way
> He was right, dead right as he sped along
> But he is just as dead as if he was wrong!

Win

This is an approach favoured by many people in business today. They are so eager to win at all costs that the feelings of the other person become totally irrelevant. If the other person wins also, good luck to them and if they lose – that's just too bad.

Regrettably, our profession breeds this mentality and admittedly, many salespeople are successful by just moving from sale to sale. I believe there is a better way and I can only encourage you to think win/win – if only for the personal satisfaction of knowing that you did the job the way it should be done!

Win/win or no sale

This concept is very popular, particularly among family members and close friends. Everyone has to agree on a family holiday location or else the family just don't go at all. It is frequently becoming a feature of contracts of employment where both parties agree the basis for the working relationship and unless both are satisfied there is no deal.

It is a favourable alternative to win/win and many companies will find themselves adding the win/win or no deal philosophy in an effort to improve management/staff relations. These same principles are of major benefit to the professional salesperson and are sometimes used thus:

> Mr Customer, I know you are concerned about spending so much money on a new product, however on the basis of our discussions I am satisfied that it is precisely what you require. Within one week of using the product you will know if it is correct for your business. If you are satisfied I will present you with my invoice. If not, I shall have it removed at no expense to you or your company. Is that a reasonable offer?

Win/win

The motivation of win/win people is based on their understanding of what this frame of mind can achieve:

- it helps us to create a cooperative rather than a competitive selling environment
- it is not my way or your way – it is our way
- that all solutions and agreements will be mutually beneficial
- that all parties feel positively committed to the action plan
- if we can sincerely adopt a win/win attitude, constantly seek to assure our customers that sales will not be achieved at their expense, we will get sales where others will fail.

People who follow the creed of win/win think in terms of: 'How can I communicate this in such a way as to ensure both of us benefit.' It may not always be possible to achieve but a win/win approach should be the ultimate aim of all our communication with others. Win/win personalities who suffer poor service would probably comment: 'I have been dealing with your company for many years and I have always been more than happy with the service you provide. Because I place a high value on our relationship I thought it important to bring a recent incident to your attention.'

A win/win personality who receives a dirty glass in a bar would probably say quietly and out of the earshot of other customers: 'This glass is not up to your usual high standards, I wonder would you mind changing it please.'

Compare this approach to the win/lose mentality: In an angry voice to a member of staff: 'Would you drink out of this filthy glass yourself?'

Remember that everything we do in association with others is highly contagious. If I am polite and courteous to you, there is an obligation on your part to respond in like manner. If I threaten or make demands, will it motivate you into positive action?

A thorough understanding of the principles of win/win can help to improve motivation in the work–place, increase professionalism in selling and create a more harmonious relationship with loved ones.

Stephen R Covey, in his excellent book, *The 7 Habits of Highly Effective People,* devotes an entire chapter to this important subject. Every salesperson should build up a library of good reference material and this book has many useful ideas that can be applied to selling.

TURNING CONFLICT INTO WIN/WIN

Because our profession brings us into contact with so many people, inevitably, there will be sporadic moments of frustration and anger. How we deal with these situations influences not only the resolution of the problem, but our continuing relationship with the 'offender'. It is very human to want to 'let off steam' but we must not lose sight of the objective, which is to resolve the problem.

We all know that conflict can take place at any time and in the worst possible circumstances. Plan your response to these moments in advance and sell yourself on the benefits of a more assertive approach. It is very simple.

- Never try to handle a difficult situation when you are upset or angry. If you do you will only make a bad situation worse.
- Revisit the situation after you have calmed down, in private and at a time of your choosing.
- Give win/win reasons for bringing the situation to the other person's attention.
- Explain – do not complain. Avoid making judgements or personalizing your remarks. Try to explain, in a passive manner, exactly what you perceive the problem to be.
- Avoid negative observations about people – talk about the system or a breakdown in communication.
- Give the other person a full opportunity to respond.

- If the response is satisfactory – be gracious.
- If the response is not totally satisfactory – start by summarizing points on which you agree and discuss remaining issues.
- If the conversation does not resolve all the difficulties – agree to revisit at another time!

Remember that attitudes are highly contagious and remember the old adage: 'A man convinced against his will is of the same opinion still.' Of one thing we can be certain: we can never force our ideas on others: the more we try the greater the resistance. Do you recall Aesop's fable of where the wind and the sun argued over who was the stronger?

> The wind challenged the sun: Do you see that man down there? I can make him take off his coat quicker than you can! The sun agreed to go behind a cloud and let the wind blow up a storm. But the more the wind blew the more firmly the old man held on to his coat. Eventually, the wind gave up and the sun came out from behind the cloud and smiled warmly on the old man. Within a short time the old man wiped his brow, took off his coat and went peacefully on his way. The sun knew the secret, friendliness and courtesy are always stronger than force and fury.

Acquiring the habit of applying these skills is a lot easier than it seems and when you consider the perils of doing it any other way, your motivation to practice it will increase!

TALK TO PEOPLE AS IF THEY ARE YOUR FRIENDS

The way we communicate with people is greatly influenced by our perceptions of where these people fit into our social and commercial network. Invariably, we group others into one of five areas – seniors; juniors; equals; opponents; friends.

If we perceive people as being senior to us, our body language tends to be subservient, our manner and tone of voice takes on an air of diplomacy and our words are carefully chosen. When we talk with subordinates our communication manner tends to be the exact opposite. If people's views differ from ours we tend to see them as opponents and subconsciously try to 'better' their argument.

However, when we see people as friends all our communication tends to be more consistent with the spirit of win/win. We talk politely and listen actively. There are no social or commercial barriers to poison the atmosphere. If we can achieve a friend–to–friend style of communication with all our contacts – particularly customers – we will be successful in any market conditions.

SEPARATE PERSONALITY FROM CHARACTER

In my experience, too many people fall into the 'either/or' personality trap of liking or disliking people and in selling this is definitely a mistake.

If you turned on the TV and you couldn't get a picture on a particular channel, undoubtedly, you would search for a another station. You wouldn't sit there all night looking at a distorted picture. Using the same analogy with person to person, why spend all your time looking only at negative traits when people obviously have better ones?

In communicating with others always treat behaviour and attitude as distinctly separate from personality and character. Recognize that it is only an aspect of the person's behaviour that you find irritating – not the person.

Try to bear in mind that people's better traits are like the iceberg – most of them are hidden beneath the surface.

PEOPLE SKILLS

One thing is certain, it you choose to work in this profession you will need to appraise yourself constantly on people skills.

- Be aware of the difference between a punishment and a correction. A punishment is given in public with the intention of humiliating. A correction is given in private with calmness and sincerity and with the intention of helping the offender.
- If you must knock somebody else's idea, do it gently, never maliciously and then only when you can come up with a better one yourself.
- Try to create an atmosphere in which others never feel threatened or manipulated.
- Never miss an opportunity to say something positive to others on their achievements, no matter how small or insignificant it may appear. Avoid being a John Blunt, the painter of the worst picture.
- Never back down from a commitment. Promises made should be kept, regardless of cost or personal embarrassment.
- Make a point of being tolerant. It's nice to be important but more important to be nice. Bring others into the 'team' by asking their advice and opinions.
- Be upright and honest in your dealings. Let others know that they are dealing with someone they can trust. Develop a reputation for being fair and just in your appraisal of others.
- Show by example and never expect others to do what you wouldn't do yourself. Avoid comparing one with another and don't expect anybody to imitate the ideals of another.
- Be a comfortable person to be with. Cultivate the quality of being stimulating and interesting and remember that a smile is the shortest distance between two people.
- Learn and use the names of supposedly unimportant people. Try to catch them doing something right. Compliment and encourage often but avoid flattery.

AVOID THE THREE Cs

If you want to destroy people, the working atmosphere, your relationships with loved ones and fail big time in selling, just master the habit of: criticizing, condemning, and complaining.

Even their occasional use is guaranteed to create tension, anger, resentment, retaliation and a highly contagious negative environment – all the usual ingredients for poison! A simple change of approach from 'this is not a criticism' to 'may I make an observation' can make a world of difference to how receptive people are to your message.

Admit your mistakes

It is not an expression we hear too often. Taking responsibility is a very important selling skill. Passing the buck or cries of 'it's not my fault' are common in our profession and guaranteed to totally frustrate a customer. Having the humility to say: 'I'm sorry, I was wrong', or 'It was entirely my fault', is a sign of strength, not weakness, and an admirable quality in people. Professional salespeople make mistakes – mediocre salespeople make excuses. One sure way to earn people's respect is to accept responsibility for your own actions.

Some time ago, as a sales manager, I was addressing a sales team. A heated debate took place between me and one of the salespeople, which culminated in me accusing him of submitting late reports. He left the office in a very angry mood, protesting his innocence but I was comforted in the knowledge that I had postmark evidence to back me up.

Later that morning my secretary told me that she had given me incorrect information and the salesperson in question had sent his reports exactly as he claimed. This incident occupied my thoughts for the entire weekend. Having considered the options I decided to do what I would like my manager to do for me. On Monday morning at our regular sales meeting I said: 'On Friday morning, I accused you of misrepresentation – it now transpires that you were right and I was wrong. As I accused you in front of your colleagues I would now like to apologize in front of your colleagues.'

Five years later when I was leaving the company, he came to me and said that of all the incidents that took place in his career, that has been the most notable. Not only had it done a lot for our relationship, but the anger he felt on coming in to work was replaced with a burst of sustained motivation.

The power of encouragement

Recognition serves as the greatest means of encouragement. There are few people, if any, who have ever achieved anything worthwhile without the understanding and kindness of someone who believed in them. We would never have heard of Charles Dickens but for the encouraging words of his first publisher. Another famous author was on the verge of suicide when his teacher told him he had a talent for writing – his name was HG Wells.

Consider the power of these statements:

- 'You really did a great job.'
- 'You have a very special talent for this kind of work.'
- 'I like the way you dress; you are always so neat and tidy.'
- 'I am delighted we are working together on this.'
- 'I appreciate all your efforts.'
- 'It's great to have you on the team.'

There is not a person in this world that does not want a kind word of appreciation or a sincere compliment. Writing a special note to a customer to thank him or her for the business can do much to maintain a positive relationship. Thanking your company for investing money in your development will be noted with enthusiasm. Showing appreciation to loved ones for their patience and support can help to sustain much needed motivation.

Seek the advice of others

Some of the most powerful statements in human relations are: 'May I ask your advice on an idea that I am working on?'; 'I would really appreciate your views'; or 'what is your opinion?'

This is what happened when two former delegates asked for someone's advice. Clem, a college graduate, relates the following:

> I arrived at my local squash club to be informed by a stern looking lady that my membership had expired and I couldn't use the centre until I had paid my annual fee. Not having the money on me I resigned myself to waiting for my friends who had gone to get changed. Without thinking, I found myself in conversation with the receptionist and mentioned that I was considering buying a new squash racquet and which type would she advise me to buy. She produced from below the counter her own racquet and gave me a complete rundown on its benefits.
>
> I must have impressed her with my interest because she suggested that I should try it and I said I would, just as soon as I paid my fee. She insisted that I should forget the fee for that night and I had an entertaining evening free of charge.
>
> When I thought about it afterwards, I was convinced that her change of attitude was a direct result of asking her advice. The sequel to this story is that since then she has become my lawyer, my doctor, my career guidance teacher, my priest and a host of other people and I never miss an opportunity to ask her advice or opinion on anything. I have been playing there for six months and I still haven't paid my fee!

Martin was another person who wrote to me. He had been thinking of buying a camera, so he approached a photographer friend and asked for his advice on making a purchase. He goes on to say:

> He produced a camera and gave me full details on why this was the right one to buy. He spent one hour explaining how it worked and then to my astonishment he handed me the camera and told to keep it as a present. If I wasn't a believer in the power of asking for opinions before the course, I am now!

It is remarkable what people achieve just by asking for opinions and advice. Asking a customer for his or her opinion on a new product on the market may help build a new relationship. By seeking the opinions of others we make them feel important and eliminate social and status barriers.

Give a little extra

Giving customers a little more than they paid for can very often lead to repeat orders. It is the spirit in which the extra is given that customers most appreciate.

One estate agent I know claims that he works entirely off referrals given to him by happy customers and explains thus. On their first evening in their new home his clients receive flowers, a bottle of wine, a specially prepared meal, the evening papers, local services directory and the temporary use of a portable TV.

He maintains that his small investment costs a fraction of what it would cost in advertising and is many times more effective. What opportunities have you got to give that little extra?

The importance of a pleasant facial expression

One of the most common faults in greeting people is the absence of a smile. In selling, a smile (without overdoing it) is a very important part of a salesperson's tool kit. It was Confucius who said: 'A man without a smiling face should not open a sweet shop', and a salesperson unable to smile should not be in selling. Considering we use more muscles when we frown than when we smile, it makes us wonder why we do not smile more often.

I know of one outstandingly successful sales company who has a definite policy on interviewing, if the interviewee does not smile as they walk into the room they will not get the job! They work on the principle that if you have problems smiling you have no business talking to their customers.

If you look at it this way, you will meet 20, 50 or perhaps 100 people every day and every one of them will have their day brightened or darkened by the tone and manner of your greeting.

Be positive and enthusiastic

The sales profession by its very nature will bring you into contact with all types of people. In general they will all have one thing in common: problems. Unknown to ourselves, we can actually depress the customer with remarks such as: 'Isn't it a lousy day?', or 'I heard that factory up the road is closing down.'

While it may be a great way to get the customer talking, it is hardly likely to do anything for his or her morale. Customers will only buy when they are motivated to do so – not when they are in the depths of depression. It is our role to find solutions to their problems and only an enthusiastic and positive approach will achieve this.

Be courteous

Courtesy is a contagious and powerful sales tool. However, too often in our profession there is a distinct lack of this important quality. Empty promises such as 'I'll phone you back in five minutes' are infuriating, particularly when you are the victim.

Companies spend fortunes advertising their products or service. Yet when the customer rings up or calls in, the salesperson sometimes fails to extend the courtesy and professionalism the customer has been led to expect. This anonymous writer put it very well when he explained:

> I'm the fellow who goes into a restaurant, sits down and waits patiently while the staff do everything but take my order.
>
> I'm the fellow who goes into a department store and stands quietly while the sales clerks finish their little chit–chat.
>
> I'm the fellow who drives into a filling station and never blows his horn, but waits while the attendant finishes his comic book.
>
> Yes… you might say I'm a good guy – but do you know who else I am?
>
> I'm the fellow who never comes back!… and it amuses me to see you spending thousands of pounds trying to get me in there… when I was there in the first place and all you had to do was treat me with a little courtesy!

Selling is a highly skilled profession with great emphasis placed on skills. It is so important, however, not to lose sight of the fact that this profession is customer–oriented. Basically, we are in the business to solve our customers' problems.

WORK HARDER AT REMEMBERING PEOPLE'S NAMES

The ability to remember people's names and to use them is an important skill not only in selling but in every profession where people's support is essential. One American newspaper considers it so important to get people's names right that the journalists lose a day's pay for spelling a name incorrectly. Consider these important points.

The most important possession we have is our names and no–one will ever be offended with checking its spelling or pronunciation. Selling is all about attention to detail, if you cannot get the customer's name right, what other important details will you miss?

Gerry is a sales executive with a plant machinery company with whom I discussed the importance of getting people's names right. A few days later, he met a customer, made his presentation and was asked for a quotation in writing. This customer was a Gaelic speaker and introduced himself by his Gaelic name. Before Gerry submitted the proposal, he made a point of researching the Gaelic spelling of the customer's name. He got the order, which was worth £50,000, and the most significant detail was what the customer said: 'There was little to choose between all three proposals, but I must admit that you were the only one who got my name right!'

Moral: If the person has an unusual name, make sure you get it right: you may be the only one who bothered. On the other hand, if your rival gets the name right and you get it wrong, it might cost you the order.

The following are some helpful hints on remembering people's names:

- When being introduced to someone, make sure you hear the name properly.
- Do not be embarrassed about asking someone to repeat or spell their name – most people will be pleased you were interested enough to ask.
- Use the person's name as often as is appropriate during the discussion.
- Repeat the name to yourself during the conversation.
- On parting, use the name again.
- Most important of all, having met new acquaintances, mentally review their names when you get a quiet moment.
- Practise remembering the names of people who work with your customer, such as receptionists and secretaries.

Remember, there is no such thing as a bad memory, just an untrained one. It is possible in a very short time to improve your retention dramatically, by applying these basic memory skills.

Skills for improving memory

One point raised constantly in discussions is this inability to remember people's names. While there are many ways to improve memory, unless you can convince people they do not have a bad memory in the first place, it is unlikely they will believe that any technique will work.

According to memory experts, if at the age of 21 you were to write down everything you can possibly remember about your past experience it would take you approximately 2500 years. Not bad for an average memory!

The use of mnemonics

Mnemonics are an aid to memory. If you wanted to remember how many days there are in April you would probably say to yourself 'thirty days hath September, April, June and November'. That is what is known as a mnemonic. If you were asked to name the five great lakes, the word 'Homes' would give great assistance:

H – Huron, O – Ontario, M – Michigan, E – Eerie, and S – Superior.

People use mnemonics to assist in public speaking and they are particularly helpful to anybody trying to remember vital information.

For salespeople AIDA has always stood for attention, interest, desire and action – the steps involved in negotiating a sale. In selling, the use of mnemonics is encouraged because not only does it aid learning, it also reinforces the message. In many cases these mnemonics are never forgotten.

Your ability to retain and recall information will be greatly enhanced if you associate new data with information you already have or understand. For example, Mount Fujiyama is 12,365 feet high. Remembering Fuji in terms of 12 calendar months and 365 days in the year should help you recall the statistic at will.

The calendar system

Let us start by improving your ability to remember dates. By learning12 digits in sequence you have a mental calendar of a certain year. Let us take the year 2000 as an example. Study the following numbers and learn them in the proper sequence. The best way to do it is to learn three first, then six, then nine, and finally 12: 265; 274; 263; 153.

Once these numbers are indelibly planted in your brain, you have a calendar for the year 2000. Each of these 12 numbers represents the first Sunday of each month of the year, ie 265 is January, February and March, 274 is April, May and June, and so on.

If you wanted to establish what day the 6 March was, for example, knowing that the first Sunday is the 5th you could easily work out that the 6th must be a Monday. It should take no more than ten minutes to learn the system completely. You can have great fun at parties demonstrating your incredible feats of memory. Use the same system for other years. The sequence of numbers will obviously change from year to year, however the sequence will repeat itself in year eight.

Communications

As a memory test, try to remember the following list of 14 words: open–mindedness; common sense; manners; names; illustration; courtesy; simplicity; understanding; observation; memory; tolerance; integrity; naturalness; attitude.

Without reading any further, how many can you remember? Was it difficult to remember four, ten, or the entire 14? Now, without looking back at the list, write down the word 'communications' and use each letter as an aid to remembering the 14 words (one letter for the start of each word). There should be a marked improvement.

The 'link' system of memory

Have a look at the following list of objects and then see how many you can remember in their proper sequence: orange; lighthouse; ballroom; deckchairs; camera; table lamp; balloon; washing machine; ladder; soap powder.

In order for memory skills to work, everything must be exaggerated out of all proportion to what it really is. The bigger, more colourful and more amusing the idea, the more chance you have of remembering it. Try to remember these objects by using the 'link' method.

First of all, visualize an orange, the biggest that you have ever seen, give it as much detail as you possibly can, and have it standing on the floor in front of you, pushing up against the ceiling.

Next imagine cutting into the orange and inside the orange is a lighthouse with lights flashing and the waves crashing into the surrounding rocks. Make the picture as vivid as possible. Imagine yourself walking inside the lighthouse and you find the biggest ballroom that you have ever seen: hear the music, see the people.

As you look round you begin to notice two deckchairs, the biggest you have ever seen, dancing with one another, and people are standing around applauding them and taking photographs with cameras. Look at these amazing cameras flashing, thousands of them. But then you notice that the flashes on the camera are different, they are all using table lamps, switching them on and off each time they take a picture. Suddenly all the cameras and table lamps explode and everything mushrooms into a massive balloon with all its colours.

When the balloon hits the ceiling it bursts with a loud bang and out of it come thousands of washing machines, floating slowly towards the ground. You walk up to the washing machines, which are twice your size, and climb on a ladder to look inside. Your feet keep slipping off the ladder as you try to look into the washing machine and you end up in a sea of soap powder.

Now write them all down in their proper sequence without looking back. Most people find they can remember every one of them with little difficulty. You may never need to use this system, but practising it does help your confidence in memory retention, and that is one of the more important aspects of developing a powerful memory.

Special exercise

Take a sheet of paper and draw a line down the centre from top to bottom. On the left hand side write down all of the positive qualities that you admire in others, things that people do or say that motivate and inspire you to positive action.

On the right hand side write down all the de–motivating traits that you have encountered in your life or career, for example, personality aspects that you find offensive or unacceptable in other people.

Take a highlighter and endorse all the positive and negative traits that you sincerely believe you possess. Make a positive decision to work on eliminating all the negatives. If you find these traits offensive there is a very real chance that others will also. Work with determination to develop new skills and accentuate the positives that you already possess

Take another sheet of paper and select someone who plays a special part in your life. Take as much time as you require writing down all of the special qualities that you believe that person possesses. Complete this exercise before you read any further.

How many points did you come up with? five?, ten? or even 15? The purpose of the exercise is to make you think:

How long is it since you told them that? How would they feel if they knew how you felt about them? How much motivation would you get by telling them? When are you going to tell them?

TEN KEY POINTS IN WINNING PEOPLE'S SUPPORT

- Remember you can make more friends in two months by being really interested in them than you can in two years by trying to get them interested in you.
- Would you like to have yourself as a boss, a friend, a spouse or a salesperson?
- Are you your No 1 rival? – is your own attitude costing you sales?
- Practising the principles win/win helps create a cooperative selling environment.
- Talk to people as if they were friends – not rivals, juniors or superiors.
- Avoid the three Cs, criticism, condemning and complaining.
- Work harder at remembering people's names.
- Try to turn conflict into win/win – explain, don't complain.
- Be encouraging – showing appreciation builds motivation and is usually returned.
- Give a little extra – a small investment of time or money can pay large dividends.

4

Establishing and Maintaining a Competitive Edge

People do not buy products, they buy the idea behind the product. Your ability to communicate this concept will have a direct bearing on your ability to succeed in selling.

This chapter will concentrate on the skills that are needed to:

- translate your expert knowledge of your product into customer benefits
- create positive images that will motivate people to buy
- uncover your unique selling points and apply them to your selling proposition
- deal with the sensitive area of competition.

THE IMPORTANCE OF PRODUCT KNOWLEDGE

Product knowledge is often taken for granted, yet the salesperson's credibility comes under scrutiny most when discussing or demonstrating the product. Product knowledge alone does not guarantee a successful sales career; but salespeople who establish themselves as experts will win the respect of the buyer and in many cases, the order along with it.

Comprehensive product knowledge covers six main areas:

1. Product features.
2. Product performance.
3. Price compared with competition.
4. Product construction.
5. Knowledge of the market.
6. Customer–related product benefits.

Product features – what it is

Any product has many features. Even an everyday item such as a pencil has features ranging from the non–toxic paint to the type and quality of the lead. The non–toxic paint may be of greater interest to a mother than it will be to an architect and the quality of the lead will be of more importance to the architect than it will be to a mother. It is important, however, that you uncover all the features of your product and cultivate the habit of selling the idea behind the feature.

Product performance – what it does

In some respects this category of product knowledge is the most important. If the salesperson cannot demonstrate how the product will solve the customer's problems, satisfy demands or needs, it is unlikely he or she will make a sale.

Many salespeople can explain how their product meets general needs; however, the professional goes one step further and demonstrates how the product is going to satisfy the customer's specific requirements. Obtaining precise specifications from the customer comes from professional fact–finding skills (see Chapter 6).

Price compared to competition

Customers raise price objections when they do not know the product's value. In order to counteract this we must have product knowledge. This means that the salesperson, when faced with the objection that his or her goods are more expensive, must be able to convince that the product is worth the extra money. On the other hand, when faced with the reverse problem – that products must be inferior because they are lower in price – he or she has to prove through product knowledge that the quality claimed does, in fact, exist.

Product construction

As the customer and the product designer are unlikely to meet, the only way the buyer can understand how the product is put together is through the salesperson. Understanding this part of product knowledge is of significant value when faced with customer objections such as: what materials are used? How is it assembled? How is it transported?

This is all valuable information. An increase in the cost of raw materials may eventually find its way to the selling price of your product: when this is explained to the customer, he or she may accept a price increase more readily. Apart from the background knowledge of the manufacturing process, you must be able to explain: your firm's service; distribution; and credit policy.

A total understanding of the company's procedure for granting credit helps to explain credit terms. Knowledge of shipping procedures might help to explain why a customer has to wait an extra week for delivery. The salesperson's ability to explain: buying and selling terms; the limits of what is covered under guarantee; and what is not covered under warranty, can be most important in making sales. A high number of service calls and customer complaints arise because products are used incorrectly. In many cases these could have been avoided by a little extra explanation by the salesperson.

Knowledge of the market

Several trade magazines cover practically every type of business. Salespeople should keep themselves up to date with: what is happening in the industry; market trends and forecasts; new ideas and new products coming on the market; and competitive activity.

Keeping yourself informed may give you a valuable advantage over competitors. Knowledge of your competitors is as important as any other branch of product knowledge because if you do not understand the competition, you are indirectly helping them.

The acquisition, application and regular updating of product knowledge is a tremendous confidence–builder for the salesperson, not only in meeting objections, but also in his or her attempts to command the customer's respect. The professional salesperson knows there is no substitute for knowledge, for nothing can hide ignorance.

Customer–related product benefits

A survey carried out on salespeople from all over Europe found that only one in eight actually expressed a benefit during the sale; all others sold features. It is the salesperson's job to determine the customer's reasons for buying and, through skill and product knowledge, to coordinate the product benefits with the customer's buying motives.

Bear in mind that a benefit must:

- solve a customer problem
- save time or money
- increase productivity or profits
- improve image or prestige
- satisfy a particular customer need.

These are the key points of your sales presentation; this is, the customer's motivation for buying. The real benefit of buying a bigger copier is to increase efficiency or reduce costs. It is not good enough to say that the copier is faster; we must also explain the corresponding benefit.

SELL THE SIZZLE – NOT THE STEAK!

In the selling process, the product is of secondary importance. The primary factor is the idea behind the product, the purpose the product fulfils. For example:

- we do not sell calculating machines, we sell speed, accuracy and efficiency
- we do not sell encyclopaedias, we sell career success and personal development.

A clear understanding of the need to sell ideas is crucial. Charles Revlon of Revlon Cosmetics put it in a nutshell when he said: 'In the factory we manufacture cosmetics but in the drug store we sell hope.'

To encourage you to start selling ideas, look at the following products and fill in the right–hand column.

We do not sell	*We do sell*
furniture	*comfort and style*
cars	*transport, status*
TVs	*entertainment*
insurance	*protection, security, investment*
double glazing	*?*
video tapes	*?*
cameras	*?*

garden furniture ?

clothes ?

CDs ?

What ideas do you sell?

UNCOVER NEEDS, BUT WANTS ARE MORE IMPORTANT!

Throughout my career, successive sales professionals have always highlighted the importance of uncovering the buyers' needs. Few if any have ever stressed one other salient point – what the customer wants. It is essential to understand that:

- everything we need to buy tends to be price negative
- everything we want to buy is price positive.

For example, price will not be the main consideration when buying your dream car but the cost of insuring it may appear outrageous. Why? We want the car but we need the insurance. The same principle applies to a new television, the license fee will appear expensive at any price.

SELL THE RESULTS OF WHAT YOUR PRODUCT CAN DO!

The way we describe our service can have an interesting effect on customer perception of price positive or negative. If I were to tell my customers that I am in the training business, most people will view it as an expense. On the other hand, if I tell them I am in the business of increasing sales, it's looked on as an investment and price is no longer the deciding factor.

Try to cultivate the habit of selling the results of what your product or service can offer and you will be pleasantly surprised how much more interested customers will be in talking to you!

Emotional appeal

It is important to understand what motivates the customer to buy your products. Some years ago, Harvard Business School carried out research with the top buyers in the US to uncover what proportion of a buying decision was based on emotion and what proportion on logic. It came up with the staggering result that 84 per cent of all decisions are based on grounds of emotion!

You may have difficulty in accepting that figure until you consider that the biggest decision most people make in their lives is whether to marry someone. Is this decision based on emotion or logic?

THE CUSTOMER'S MOTIVATION FOR BUYING

Every time we buy something, we do so because it satisfies a need or desire. When we are expressing the benefits of our product to the customer, we must appeal to his or her dominant motive for buying. Buying motives fall into two groups, emotional and rational.

Emotional reasons for buying are:

- fear – of competition, of being left behind
- envy – of others' successful achievements
- vanity – recognition by others of having made a wise decision
- love – approval of colleagues, family and friends
- entertainment – enjoyment, relaxation, and so on
- sentiment – family tradition, local company
- pride – being associated with a successful project

- pleasure – derived from the appearance of the new purchasing, design, etc.

Rational reasons for buying are:

- profit – increased efficiency, less wastage
- health – less hazardous to heart, less strain
- security – well established firm, brand names, proven track record
- utility – easier to use, less effort, time saving, etc.
- caution – fewer service calls, durability, long life, and so on.

Having discovered the customer's problem areas, we can give him or her added reasons for buying by tying in product benefit with buying motives.

UNCOVER YOUR UNIQUE SELLING POINTS

Salespeople will find it difficult to differentiate their products from rivals unless they stress the 'unique' aspects of what they are selling. It will be a very poor product or service that doesn't have at least one Unique Selling Point (USP). In other words, something of value to the buyer, that nobody else in your industry can or will provide. When you know what these unique points are, make sure the customer hears about them! Your USPs could be:

- a quicker service, more experienced personnel, or longest established company
- a product feature which no other manufacturer can match
- a money–back guarantee, extended warranty, or free trial period
- the colour, size, shape or price of the product
- a free help line, or on–site maintenance
- the only product manufactured locally.

Your USPs must be highlighted against the selling points of your competitors so that you can answer the buyer's unasked question: 'What can you offer me that the others cannot?'

The advantage to you as a salesperson is if the customer perceives a real benefit from your USP – you have a great chance of getting the business! Astonishingly most salespeople don't bother about USPs, this gives you a significant selling edge.

Confidence plays a major role in buying. Salespeople who truly understand the strengths and weaknesses of their rivals' products will be a great comfort to buyers who depend on salespeople to educate them.

As a special exercise, list the unique selling points of your product; list the unique selling points of your service; and list the unique points of your company.

DEALING WITH THE SENSITIVE AREA OF COMPETITION

It is rare for a customer to make a purchase without first having checked out the competition. Invariably salespeople will be confronted with questions, comparisons or objections raised at the selling interview. How salespeople handle the sensitive area of competition may have a bearing on who gets the order.

One of the most unprofessional things that a salesperson can do is knock the competition. Some salespeople go to another extreme and out of respect for their rivals they inadvertently hand them over the business. Some important points to bear in mind (and practice constantly) are the following:

- let your rivals do their own selling
- treat fellow professionals with respect
- watch your body language when competitors are mentioned

- when rivals knock your company – take it as a compliment
- keep the standards of the industry up
- do not single out a competitor for special mention.

Let your rivals do their own selling

Some time ago a colleague responded to a telephone inquiry, signed up a lucrative contract, and on leaving asked the customer where he got our name. The customer replied: 'From one of your rivals'. We would not have got the order if our rival had not mentioned us. Why he singled us out we will never know, but I will be happy if he continues to do so.

If a competitor is mentioned, pay polite attention and say something like, 'Very nice people' or 'I know the company' or, 'Yes, I've heard of them.' By making such comments you are acknowledging their existence without committing yourself one way or the other. Why give free advertising, particularly to your competitors?

Treat fellow professionals with respect

The golden rule of selling is 'Never knock the competition', even in the most subtle manner such as: 'Never heard of them', or 'I never knock the competition – no matter how bad it is.'

There is usually only one interpretation of a salesperson slating a rival company – he or she is afraid of them! That is all the buyer needs to be convinced of where to place the order.

Mind your body language when competitors are mentioned

When a buyer mentions the competition it is understandable that the salesperson may interpret it as a threat to getting the order and become physically agitated. It's easy to become defensive and the customer may well think, 'I wonder why she is so worried about them; maybe I should check them out.'

It takes a lot of training and self–discipline to cope with competition on an unemotional basis. Buyers are professionals and some quite deliberately observe the salesperson's reaction when competitors are introduced into the discussion. Anticipate that a rival's name will be brought up, and practice a more passive response.

When rivals knock your company, take it as a compliment

It would be quite understandable if you over–reacted to a suggestion from the customer that a rival was making wild accusations about your company. If this happens do not fall into the trap of replying with comments like: 'The things I could tell you about that crowd', or 'People in glass houses shouldn't throw stones.'

While such reactions may be understandable, they are professionally unacceptable, and likely to work against you.

Keep up the industry standards!

From personal experience and customer comments it is easy to categorize rivals as top class or poor. Some salespeople dwell too much on drawing comparisons between their own companies and the bad ones. Usually this is a mistake because it encourages the customer to perceive the overall standard in your industry as poor. And why? Because salespeople keep telling them! Tell customers how good you are, not why they shouldn't deal with everybody else!

Don't single out a competitor for special mention

As an experienced salesperson and out of respect for my rivals (which was the first thing I learned about selling) I went to the other extreme. To demonstrate my lack of fear of the competition when a rival's name came up I would say, 'Oh yes, we are very familiar with them. In fact they are our "arch rivals".'

Having lost a number of orders I began to ask myself why the buyers were giving orders to salespeople who, at the time of my interview, had not spoken to the customers. It took me too long to realize I was giving the customer vital competitive information which was undermining my efforts. Ever since then I have handled the question differently by stating: 'Mr Customer, we have 27 other companies competing with us in the market–place. All are taking a share of the market because they are all very good companies.'

By answering in this way, I am improving or maintaining the customer's perception of the industry. Furthermore, I hope the customer is saying to himself: 'I have not got time to look at 27 other companies. This does not look too risky and if this guy makes it easy for me to buy, I might as well get this out of the way and get on to something else.'

The ultimate sign of the professional salesperson is one who can confidently deal with competition and accept gracefully that you cannot get all the business – if you did, selling would lose all its excitement and drama!

TEN KEY POINTS FOR GENERATING NEW BUSINESS

- Your credibility as an expert comes under scrutiny most with product knowledge.
- Sell the sizzle not the steak – remember to sell the idea behind the product!

- We do not sell furniture – we sell comfort!
- Sell the results of what your product can do – this converts expense into investment!
- Everything we need is price negative – everything we want is price positive!
- The only way to differentiate your product from your rivals is to highlight your USP.
- As most people ignore their USP this gives you an advantage.
- Eighty-four per cent of all decisions are based on grounds of emotion.
- Find out what it is that motivates your customers to buy your products!
- When rivals knock your products – you are beginning to worry them!

5

Establishing a Positive Selling Environment

One thing salespeople throughout the world have in common is that we all sell to people. We do not sell to factories or warehouses or stores, we sell to people with feelings and emotions. Losing an order to a rival is painful, losing an order through a lack of sensitivity or care is the selling equivalent of committing hari kari. In this session we will deal with:

- how badly chosen words can cost you a sale
- how to read the essentials of customer body language
- how to create a positive first impression.

UNDERSTAND HOW BADLY CHOSEN WORDS CAN COST YOU A SALE!

Even if *you* are a perfect communicator you still have to deal with all the rest of us who are not perfect! It is important to be conscious of the barriers to effective communication:

Exaggeration

It is important in your enthusiasm not to oversell the benefits of your products. The use of superlatives should be avoided. Claiming that your product is the finest', the best or the biggest is likely to be disbelieved – unless you can provide hard factual evidence.

Vagueness and generalities

It is easy to fall into the trap of using statements such as: 'Most companies have found...'; 'It is generally accepted...'; 'Most people agree...'; or 'According to the experts...'

It is acceptable to use these statements provided they are backed up by the relevant knowledge, experts name and the facts.

Egocentric language

Certain expressions discourage people from buying so avoid saying things such as: 'If I were you'; 'Think about what I said'; 'My advice would be'; or 'If you want my opinion'.

Any of these expressions could create a negative selling environment. Changing 'I think' to 'what do you think' could be the difference between selling and not selling.

Buzz words and jargon

Customers are not impressed when they hear salespeople use buzz words and jargon – they become confused! Similarly, using words that others may not understand is to be avoided. Mark Twain once said: 'I never write "metropolis" when I get paid the same money for writing "city".'

Give your listener a chance and consider the communication process from their point of view. A useful guideline in selling is that anything capable of being misinterpreted will be misinterpreted.

Avoid the phrases that can cost you sales

Some time ago on a sales call I witnessed a salesperson responding to a question from a customer by saying, 'without getting too technical'. The customer barked back angrily: 'Its OK to get technical – I am an engineer.' Perhaps the salesperson's lack of sensitivity may account for the fact that we did not get the business.

I list here a number of frequently overused phrases in selling – along with their possible interpretations – many of which are extremely offensive and have 'no sale' written across them. Please believe me these phrases have cost salespeople sales and continue to do so:

'With all due respects'
('Thinking very little of you as I do')
Better: avoid it like the plague.
'You are entitled to your opinion/I disagree with you!'
('You are wrong! Use these expressions and you simply will not sell!')
Better: show respect for others' opinions.
'Without getting too technical/ To put this in simple terms/ I hope this doesn't go over your head'
('You are such a fool that I am going to explain this to you in baby talk')
Better: skip it altogether.
'You have misinterpreted me'
('There was nothing wrong with the way I explained myself, you are the problem here and if only you were capable of better listening')
Better: 'I have not explained myself properly.'
'What you should do is'
('You are obviously not capable of making up your own mind')
Better: may I suggest.
'I am not interrupting you… but'
('Shut up! What I have got to say is much more important')
Better: never interrupt.

'Now don't take offence... but' or 'Don't take this personally... but'
('When was the last time that you had a bath?')
Better: avoid it altogether.
'So what you are trying to say is'
('You are obviously having problems trying to express yourself')
Better: so in other words.
'I have a better idea'
('Your idea wasn't much use, was it?')
Better: as an extension to your idea.
'I hope I am not boring you!/Without boring you any further'
('I am bored by it, everybody else is bored by it')
Better: avoid it altogether.
'I am not condemning, criticizing or complaining... but'
('That is precisely what you are about to do!')
Better: may I make an observation?

Tune into the other person's wavelength

An important aspect of our ability to communicate is talking and listening on the same 'wavelength' and understanding these wavelengths assists better communication. There are five very distinct levels:

- Level 5. Clichés – (greetings)
- Level 4. Small talk – (discussion on the weather)
- Level 3. Fact-finding and exchange of opinions – (possible conflict)
- Level 2. Emotions and feelings – (customer complaints)
- Level 1. High level dialogue – (peak communication).

Level 5: Clichés

Practically all greetings are followed up with, 'How are you?', 'Been on holiday?', 'Nice day' and so on. As we can't talk to people in clichés all day we will either end the conversation or move on to the next level. It is this level that involves the greatest number of people.

Level 4: Small talk

This includes neutral topics such as the weather or television programmes or observations about our surroundings. It is unlikely that either party will have any conflict at this level. This involves about half as many people as the cliché level.

Level 3: Fact-finding and exchange of opinions

Salespeople should make an effort to get to this level as quickly as possible, as this is where selling should take place. It involves the exchange of ideas, facts and opinions. Communication is more comfortable at this level and involves a certain amount of risk because opinions are expressed.

Level 2: Emotions and feelings

For this level to be achieved there must be an atmosphere of mutual trust and respect. It is generally reserved for a select number of friends and colleagues and members of your family. As it involves the emotions, people may open their hearts to you and it should be interpreted as a vote of confidence in your friendship. In a selling situation, while it is acceptable to express your 'feelings', beware of embarrassing the buyer by becoming emotional.

Level 1: High-level dialogue

Reserved only for the most intimate of friends or lovers. Requires the highest levels of trust between both parties, and the circle of people communicated with at this level will be few. This level can also be communicated through body language such as touching, smiling or looking.

Levels 3 and 2 are the levels that concern us most in selling and what these levels tell us is this:

- Meaningful dialogue will only take place at level three – fact-finding. So let us get there as quickly and as comfortably as the situation allows.
- While there is nothing wrong with expressing your feelings – ensure you do not embarrass the buyer by becoming emotional!
- Complaints provoke emotion and customers will be hyper-sensitive to level 5 responses 'no point in talking to me, I only work here!'

I have known salespeople to spend about 90 per cent of their precious face-to-face meeting time discussing football, golf and drama (level 4) and then wonder why they are not getting sales! Inability to empathize with customers who are angry (level 2) might also cost you business.

USE WORDS THAT SELL

The words that we use create mental images in the mind of the receiver. Images that arouse emotions (costs), imply threats (contract), frighten people (sign here) or cause a negative reaction (our product is cheaper). Our lack of sensitivity to customer moods can cost us dearly, particularly if we choose the wrong word at the wrong time. Consider some of the following phrases and words.

Avoid	*Use instead*
'Sign here please'	*'OK, the paperwork!', or 'Your approval'.*
Contract	*agreement or paperwork*
Cheaper	*less expensive, better value*
Costs	*valued at, worth, a special offer at.*

Review the words and phrases that you use with customers

and watch for reactions. If a poorly chosen word gets a negative response, it is time to find a positive alternative.

HOW TO READ THE ESSENTIALS OF CUSTOMER BODY LANGUAGE

The importance of body language should never be underestimated. Actions do speak louder than words. The ability to observe and understand the non-verbal messages we send or receive is an important skill in selling. Remember that:

- up to 90 per cent of a message is transmitted non-verbally
- when the body conflicts with the spoken word, the body is always correct
- any spontaneous movement of the hand to the face is an indication that the speaker is uncomfortable, embarrassed or not telling the truth.

Just one chapter is insufficient to cover this entire subject. However, outlined below are some of the areas of body language applicable to professional salespeople. Remember, while you are receiving messages from your customers through their body language, they too are receiving similar, revealing messages about you!

Personal space

Everyone has their own personal space which others invade at their peril. If you observe how closely you sit with intimate friends and compare it to the distance you keep from a stranger, you'll see immediately the importance of keeping your distance when you are approaching new acquaintances. The following diagram demonstrates the categories of person whom we allow to enter each of our personal spheres. The categories can be explained as follows (see Figure 5.1).

Near and distant intimate spheres (0 to 18 inches)

People protect this distance as if it were their own private sphere. We see this every day on trains and buses where people sit in the middle of the seat, or put a bag beside them, discouraging others from sitting too close. The close intimate sphere (up to 6 inches) is for people who are allowed to touch, such as partners, lovers or children. The distant intimate sphere (6 to 18 inches) is reserved for close friends. As the intimacy of the relationship decreases, so the distance increases.

Close personal sphere (1.5 to 4 feet)

This is the distance we stand from others at business seminars, parties and get-togethers.

Social sphere (4 to 10 feet)

This is the distance we allow when communication with strangers is inevitable. Most selling is done at this distance because it affords a certain amount of protection. The social sphere (4 feet) should be observed when discussing business matters with new acquaintances.

- Near intimate sphere (up to 6 inches) – partners, lovers, children, family
- Close personal sphere (1 .5 to 4 feet) – business seminars, business parties, get-togethers
- Distant intimate sphere (6 inches to 18 inches) – close friends, close colleagues, relatives
- Social sphere (4 to 10 feet) – new acquaintances, new colleagues at work, training small groups
- Public sphere (over 10 feet) – speaking to large audiences.

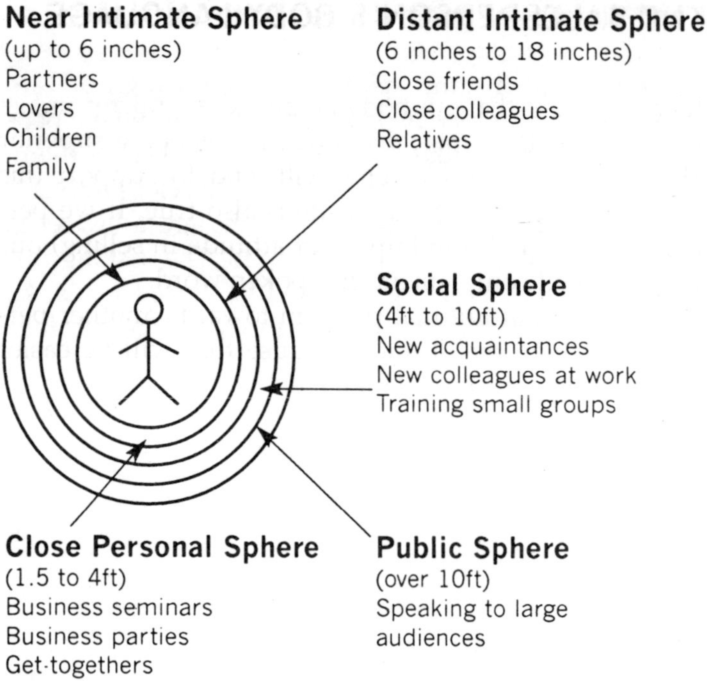

Figure 5.1 *Personal space*

Public sphere (10 to 25 ft)

This sphere is used when addressing a large group of people, such as at a social function or lecture. People who live in cities have different attitudes to personal space from those of people born and brought up on farms, for example. If you spend your working days in buses, trains, elevators and close contact with others you will feel differently towards a stranger standing four feet away from how a farmer would feel. People's sensitivity to space has to be acknowledged and observed; so keep your distance.

THE SALESPERSON'S BODY LANGUAGE

Evidence suggests that our body language is a mirror image of our thoughts. If we perceive ourselves as being superior to others, our body movements will tend to support this unspoken attitude and the opposite is also true. If we perceive others as equals (an important attitude in selling) our body signals will complement the spoken word.

If you have an attitudinal problem towards another person, try to change the attitude because that will be easier than controlling your body language.

(a)

(b)

Figure 5.2 *Examples of body language (1)*

Superior body language

Let's take some examples of superior body language often seen in manager/subordinate role. In Figure 5.2 (a) the manager is using the 'chop' and subconsciously dismissing the other person's views as being irrelevant

In Figure 5.2 (b) the steepled hands are probably a mirror image of his thoughts: 'I am in control here.' This gesture is often seen at the discipline interview. It may also be adopted up by salespeople when deflecting critical comments from a customer.

Understanding the role that body language plays in a selling situation can assist in improving communication with customers and allow us to adjust our response accordingly.

Body contact

It is perfectly acceptable for a manager to clap a subordinate on the back after a job well done, but how would you the manager react if the situation was reversed? A salesperson would need to have a good relationship with a customer to be able to touch because to do so would mean invading his or her personal space. In a selling situation, putting your arm around a customer's shoulder may communicate a closeness perceived by you but rejected by the customer. I know of one salesperson who lost a sale because he touched the customer's lapel and said: 'Nice suit'.

Shaking hands

When people shake hands many things are communicated. The weak handshake is often thought to suggest a weak character and, while we know this is untrue it may lead another to feel they can dominate you. The weak handshake might imply you are not pleased to meet the other person. Bone crushers may suggest you wish to dominate. Handshakes should be warm and strong without being 'wet fish' or knuckle-grinding. A characteristic of many salespeople is excessively strong handshakes. Regrettably, they do not communicate the image of a helpful salesperson.

Hand to face gestures

Any spontaneous movement of the hand to the face is an indication that the individual is uncomfortable, and probably lying. These gestures are a relic from childhood days. A child who does not want to hear it is time for bed will cover her ears. If there is something frightening on TV she will cover her eyes with her arms. If she tells a lie her hand will go to her mouth. As we get older, we learn to refine our reactions, but the basic attempt to conceal the lie continues.

Ask a customer: 'What are my chances of getting the order?' and he replies: 'I'd say they are pretty good', is accompanied by pulling the collar, or scratching the neck (Figure 5.3 (a)); rubbing the ear (Figure 5.3 (b)); or the eye (Figure 5.3 (c)); pretending to scratch the nose (Figure 5.3 (d)); or covering the mouth (Figure 5.3 (e)).

The implications are that the customer is lying. Why would a person who is sitting comfortably suddenly respond with these gestures? Rephrase the question and see if you get the same reaction. If you do, you will know to change your approach, the customer is not sold.

Evaluation

More positive body language is projected in Figure 5.3 (f) where the character is evaluating the message received. Interest is portrayed by sitting forward and with the index finger pointing upwards (Figure 5.3 (g)). A more critical evaluation posture is portrayed in Figure 5.3 (h); in this case the chin is resting on the hand and this may be a danger signal that your message is not being positively received. Regardless of the facial expression, a trainee taking up this posture is not giving positive attention.

Figure 5.3 *Examples of body language (2)*

Arm folding

Each movement of the body has its own expressive function, whether conscious or unconscious. If people have negative thoughts about you or your product they may fold their arms to 'shield' your unfavourable message.

Alan Pease, in his excellent book *How to Use Body Language for Power, Success and Love,* says:

> Tests carried out on two groups of students corroborated these findings. One group was asked to attend a series of talks and instructed to take up a relaxed sitting position with legs and arms uncrossed. A second group were instructed to keep their arms crossed firmly against their chests. The results showed the group who had their arms folded learned and remembered 38 per cent less than the group who had their arms unfolded, they also had more negative thoughts about the speaker and the lectures.

In a one-to-one conversation, if the other person folds his arms in the middle of your conversation (see Figure 5.4), it may well mean he disagrees, even though the facial expression and the spoken word imply otherwise. Persisting on your line of discussion may prove fruitless. Experts suggest that handing the person something or getting the person to do some task which requires a change of body language will automatically change the attitude.

Some people claim that arm folding is a comfortable way to sit, and this is a legitimate argument when the chair has no arms or there is no table on which to lean. If this is not the case however, the person is probably negative and you should alter your approach accordingly. Interestingly enough, many speakers are so conscious of the communication barriers imposed by 'arm folding' that they actually instruct delegates not to fold their arms or cross their legs during the session.

Figure 5.4 *Examples of body language (3)*

Arms folded with clenched fist

Folded arms accompanied by clenched fists suggests that the person may explode at any moment. Interesting research has been carried out on the folded arms position: the tests indicated that when the listener folds his or her arms, they are paying less attention and are likely to have more critical comments to make about the speaker.

Eye contact

Some non-verbal signals seem to be beyond any conscious control. One of these is pupil dilation. You may force yourself to look at a person's face while talking, thereby pretending to have an interest you do not feel, but you cannot consciously control the size of your pupils.

If you look into a customer's eyes just as the price is mentioned, you may see surprise at the price being lower than expected, shock at it being so high, or a neutral reaction. It may happen that the buyer will verbalize 'shock' on hearing the price only to be betrayed by lack of pupil reaction.

When a person becomes excited the pupils may dilate up to four times their normal size. On the other hand when a person is in an angry or negative mood they will contract to half their normal size.

When we are listening, our eye contact is as high as 100 per cent but when we are talking our eye contact can be as low as zero – and that does not help our skill to communicate. Beware of staring, ogling or running your eyes up and down another person. It makes others feel most uncomfortable.

The pupils will change size with the interest an individual feels. For example, if a man is looking at a woman and feels attracted to her, his pupils will dilate, and vice versa. If a poker player has an exciting hand his pupils will dilate also. Similarly if a customer is offered an interesting proposal his pupils will automatically enlarge.

Unlike many other body language signals, the attraction to the opposite sex of dilated pupils has been known for over 100 years. In the last century, the 'ladies of the night' took belladonna, a drug which dilated the pupils, to attract custom. More recently, Desmond Morris in his book *Manwatching* showed two, almost identical photographs of a young woman to a group of men. The only difference was that an artist had touched up the eye pupils in one of them. Significantly, when asked to choose their favourite, practically everybody opted for the girl with the enlarged pupils!

Facial expression

Facial expressions are the most obvious forms of non-verbal communication. However, a salesperson should remember to read the facial expression in relation to other body movements which are more reliable indicators of real feelings as they are more difficult to control

Body posture

Body language is hard to fake at any time and posture is no different. The exception to the rule, may be on the beach where a man passes an attractive woman and may consciously pull in his stomach to give a more attractive appearance.

Observing the customer's posture is obviously important, especially if he sits up in the middle of a particular point, signifying interest (see Figure 5.5 (a)). Slouching in the chair or resting the head on the palm (Figure 5.5 (b)) indicates a lack of enthusiasm for the point under discussion.

Any forward movement is usually an indication of real interest, whereas a backward movement suggests the person is withdrawing from the discussion.

Figure 5.5 *Examples of body language (4)*

Learn more about body language

Study people carefully and be aware of your own body language. Any good bookshop will provide a litany of reference material which will add to your knowledge of this important element of communication.

Body language is a fascinating area of study to which many people are devoting their time. By observing more, by improving your powers of perception and by knowing as much as possible about people, you should be able to translate more accurately your own and others' non-verbal messages.

TEN KEY POINTS IN ESTABLISHING A POSITIVE SELLING ENVIRONMENT

- Even if you are a perfect communicator – you deal with people who are not!
- Be economic with the use of superlatives – you put everything you say at risk.
- Avoid egocentric language such as 'my advice would be…'
- Customers are not impressed with jargon – they are confused.
- The words we use create mental images in the mind of the receiver.
- Avoid offensive phrases – 'with all due respects', 'I disagree with you'.
- Choose words that sell – 'value', 'agreement' and 'approval'.
- Observe body language – actions really do speak louder than words.
- Spontaneous movement of hand to face – indicates that the speaker may be lying.
- Take time out to study your own and others' body language.

6

Fact-finding: The Essential Ingredient of Successful Selling

Understandably, we all like to think that a fundamental selling procedure such as fact-finding, is something that we can do in our sleep. This is in total contrast to the buyer's view that generally, sales interviewing skills range from mediocre to very poor. If you can do this part of the selling process correctly and tie in your products' benefits with customers' needs, you will get sales where others will fail!

The purpose of this session is to develop your ability to:

- create a positive first impression
- plan a professional fact-finding meeting
- maintain and keep focused on essential information
- conduct a professional fact-finding meeting.

HOW TO CREATE A POSITIVE FIRST IMPRESSION

It can take many hours of negotiating to win a customer, and yet some salespeople are capable of disqualifying themselves in the first 60 seconds of meeting. First impressions count, as the saying goes: 'What you are shouts at me so loudly, I can't hear what you are saying!'

According to buyer research, 50 per cent of all sales perish in the first minute for one or more of the following reasons: poor preparation for the meeting; confused call objective; no apparent reason for the call; saying things like 'I just happened to be in the area'; a weak or overly strong handshake; inability to maintain eye contact; lack of confidence; pouncing back with a response; poor personal presentation; interrupting or not listening; lack of enthusiasm; knocking the competition; making smart remarks; talking too much; responding badly to questions or comments; only interested in selling the product; overstating the product's benefits; lack of interest in the customer's problems; giving the impression that you know it all; and finally, putting on the pressure.

Remember: the last thing you should do is sell

When I introduced the concept of non-technique selling I drew reference to this important issue. It is often the case that salespeople jump from their introduction to selling the product without fact-finding the customer needs. People who aim straight for the close will pick up the occasional order but they will never be as successful as the professional who recognizes the need for fact-finding.

There is another unfortunate side to this, because if the salesperson is not achieving sales it is incorrectly assumed that he or she cannot close. He or she is then given extra tuition on closing skills that only make a bad situation worse. Closing is not the difficulty here – the problem is opening the sale!

Stand out from the pack

Take a couple of moments to consider the following questions:

- How many salespeople will your customers see in one day?
- How different is your approach to that of other salespeople?
- How important is it that you should be more professional?
- If you were the customer, how would you like to be approached?

Your answers to these questions should feed your motivation to do whatever is necessary to be that little bit different. Sometimes it is something very simple that separates one person from the rest.

Recently in a restaurant, the waiter came over to me and asked that age-old question: 'Is everything all right with your meal.' Then he followed it up with: 'May I get you some more meat or vegetables?' I almost choked in surprise. That's all it takes – that little bit extra!

How many visits to close the business?

Before you visit your customer decide whether it is appropriate to try to sell your product or service in one visit. Consider the following:

- Is the buyer likely to look at other proposals?
- Will he or she need to consult colleagues before deciding?
- Is it a significant purchase?
- Does it involve major finance?
- If the answer to any of these questions is yes, you will do yourself a major disservice by trying to sell your product at one sales interview.

Look at the buying process from the customer's point of view: you would not buy equipment costing £100,000 from the first person who walked into your office. Like all sensible people you would shop around and gather all the appropriate information. If you frequently hear objections such as: I want to think it over; Leave it with me and I will get back to you; I am not going to make a decision today; you should recognize the symptoms of poor fact-finding and the one-call close. If you accept that success in selling your product is a two-call process, then absolutely no selling should take place on the first visit.

Every salesperson knows that the penalty for not selling is a change of job or career. Ironically, this constant pressure forces salespeople to double their number of calls and try and sell at every opportunity. The very suggestion that they should relax, slow down and put more effort into each individual call is received with disdain. They forget that the customer has to see other proposals and the pressure they impose for a decision actually works against them. If you are a one-call close merchant, maybe it is time to think again!

TIPS ON THE RIGHT APPROACH

Remember:

- Avoid boring and depressing conversation such as 'dreadful weather, that was terrible news this morning'. Buyers are more likely to respond positively when they are in good humour – not when they are in the depths of despair.
- Buyers are not interested in you or your company, they are only interested in what you can do for them.
- Decision-makers are busy people, they won't waste time talking to people who have nothing to offer.
- If you wish to compliment the customer on the premises or the staff make sure it is sincere. Flattery will get you nowhere in selling.
- It is absolutely essential to know something about the company you are visiting. It is blatantly unprofessional to ask: 'What exactly do you do here?'

Practise your opening statement before you enter and imagine everything going smoothly. It might be worded as follows:

> Mr Customer, it was very good of you to take the time to meet me this morning. My purpose in being here is just to do some fact finding and get information on what you are hoping to achieve by upgrading your present system. On conclusion of our meeting, I will put together some ideas for the purpose of further discussion, if, of course, I feel that my company has something to offer. If you are agreeable, may I ask you... '

If the circumstances are wrong for positive discussion ask the customer for an alternative appointment. You cannot compete with major distractions.

Avoid giving a litany of things the product can do, how big the company is, why you are the market leaders, before the customer has had time to speak. Abraham Lincoln had some valuable advice that we can all apply to selling: 'It is better to remain silent and let everybody think you are a fool than to open your mouth and remove all doubt!'

Making the customer feel comfortable

An essential part of the approach which eventually leads into conducting an effective fact-finder is making your contact feel comfortable in your presence. It is obviously important that you feel comfortable with yourself and assuming that you do:

- have a start, a middle, and a finish to what you intend to do
- have a friendly expression on your face at all times
- talk about their interests
- use the customer's name occasionally
- maintain alert body language.

As mentioned in Chapter 3, try to see the customer as a friend and not an opponent. Without overdoing it, try to communicate the image of a person who is happy with life, happy in your job and happy to meet the customer!

HOW TO PLAN A PROFESSIONAL FACT-FINDING MEETING

Produce your own pre-call preparation sheet and fill in the important details. Here is an idea as to how this document might look:

Customer profile

Name and correct spelling
Job title
Decision-making authority
Other decision-making influences
Special knowledge
Other useful information.

This is the easy part of the research and only requires a telephone call to the receptionist. Having this essential information will at least help the selling atmosphere. Getting personal details wrong will probably cost you a sale. Let's look at the perils of ignoring these fundamentals:

- You spelt the customer's name wrongly – his/her most important possession. The buyer is not impressed!
- You got the job title wrong: you promoted or demoted the customer. This embarrassed the customer.
- You assumed that he/she was the decision-maker. You just wasted your time giving a great presentation to the wrong person.
- You thought the buyer was also the user. The person with the real need wasn't invited to the meeting.
- You didn't know that the customer was a highly-qualified engineer and irritated him with unnecessary explanations.

This lack of attention to detail has probably cost you a sale and you haven't even started into the sales interview. Selling at the best of times is a difficult profession, so don't handicap yourself by ignoring the basics. On a personal level, I have an unusual surname and 90 per cent of salespeople will get it wrong. I am pleased when people go to the trouble of getting it right.

Company knowledge

What do they do?
What do they sell?
Who are their competitors?
How many people are employed?
How many branches do they have?
What other names should you know?
Who else will be involved in the discussion?
What problems do they need to resolve?

It may not be necessary to have all of this information available to you, but it is no load to carry and it is a good selling habit to develop. Figure 6.1 shows how a typical fact-finding sheet might look. Figure 6.2 shows an interview preparation checklist.

The extent of the knowledge required prior to a sales interview will depend on the impact your product or service will have on that business. For example, if you are selling paper clips, basic customer details will suffice. If you are selling a high-tech computer network, you will benefit from extensive pre-call information. To put it in a nutshell: *proper pre-call preparation prevents particularly poor presentations.*

FINDING PROBLEMS – SELLING SOLUTIONS

If a doctor prescribed medication without asking questions you would be concerned. Similarly, if you do not research the customer's needs you run the risk of prescribing an

FACT-FINDING

Interviewer ______ **Interviewee** ______ **Date** ______

Purpose of interview ______

Anticipated difficulties ______

Background information ______

Interview approach

- greeting ______
- small talk ______
- purpose ______
- probe ______

Information required ______

Pre-arranged questions (probe indirectly – why? what? where? when? etc)

- ______
- ______
- ______
- ______
- ______
- ______

Overall summary ______

Action to be taken ______

Figure 6.1 *Typical fact-finding sheet*

INTERVIEW PREPARATION: CHECKLIST

Q.1 **What is the purpose of this meeting?**

Q.2 **Who requested it?**

Q.3 **What information or research will be required in advance of the meeting?**

Q.4 **What is the background to the query or difficulty?**

Q.5 **What is the expected attitude of the interviewee?**

Q.6 **What can I say or do to create the right atmosphere?**

Q.7 **What awkward questions are likely to arise?**

Q.8 **How will I open the discussion?**

Q.9 **What action can I promise and when can I deliver?**

Q.10 **What alternative dates can I offer for follow up?**

Figure 6.2 *Interview preparation: a checklist*

inappropriate solution. You might get the sale but you will lose your credibility. Improper fact-finding is a major problem in our profession and here is just one of many examples I can quote.

As guest speaker at a computer exhibition, I carried out research to personalize the presentation. I phoned ten companies at random and told them I wanted to buy desk-top publishing equipment. This was the response.

- Eight salespeople did not ask me any questions relating to my needs. The two people who did enquire asked a total of four questions between them. Without any information of any consequence each of them launched into a sales presentation full of jargon, technical information and irrelevant product information. No-one was interested in what I wanted to produce but they had great enthusiasm for their expansion slots, drive bays, integrated single channels and the infrared wireless communications port.

Of course there were many positive aspects of each discussion but prescribing before you diagnose has 'no sale' written all over the remedy!

THE IMPORTANCE OF PROPER FACT-FINDING

Salespeople who neglect to carry out proper fact-finding may suggest top-of-the-range products when less expensive models will suffice. For example, a buyer with a printing requirement of 1000 copies per month does not need a printer capable of producing 20 times that volume. Over-selling is unprofessional, the customer feels let down and it does nothing for the image of the profession.

Underselling is in many ways more serious than overselling. Buyers are at the mercy of salespeople and depend on them to offer realistic solutions to their problems. We have all had the experience of buying a product on salespeople's recommendations only to find that the product is totally inadequate for its intended use. This usually means having to buy again and the original purchase becomes redundant.

Get the appropriate information and make suggestions on the basis of what the customer needs and not on what you would like to sell!

How much information should you give?

Before customers decide to buy, they will obviously need to know something about your company, sometimes referred to as 'rascil factors' (see below). When that information should be given is an important issue. One thing is certain, the customer does not need this information at the outset of negotiations! You will always have options open to you.

- Give a brief overview of the company and the services you will provide.
- Explain that you will give all the relevant company details when appropriate.
- If you represent a major, well-known company leave the details out for now.

Rascil factors

These are the all-important details of your product or service, summed up in the acronym RASCIL:

- reputation of your company (how long established)
- authorized products or services (brand names)
- safety features (money back guarantees)
- completeness of service (competence of staff – 24 hours' service?)
- integrity of the operation (quality certificates, ISO, etc)
- location and areas served (countrywide service).

Focus on the purpose of your call

One way to eliminate the problem associated with fact-finding is to write down your opening statement, practise it as you would a speech and include the phrases: 'The purpose of my call is...'; 'At this visit I would hope to get some information'; 'To ensure that I understand exactly what you need, may I ask you... 'This will at the very least, create a positive environment for discussion and the customer knows exactly what you intend to do.

Call the shots

Keeping control of the interview from start to finish is crucial and few salespeople get this part right. A good way to approaching this is to:

- introduce yourself and your company
- conduct a brief ice-breaker
- bridge from ice-breaking to purpose of the call
- carry out a skilful fact-finder
- summarize information obtained
- agree a date to revisit with proposal
- thank buyer for time and leave.

In the main, most buyers will be happy to give you a few moments to feel comfortable. A brief discussion about the holidays, the weekend or a game of golf is a useful ice-breaker. But remember to keep it short and sweet; you don't get paid for small talk.

This is the most crucial part of the entire interview: the first person to ask a question will take over the discussion and it is difficult to get back in control. To avoid sounding rude it is important that you bridge from whatever you are saying straight into your fact-finding; for example: 'Well, I hope you get great weather for the weekend – I am also looking forward to getting to the seaside with the family' (without inviting a response). 'I know that you have other meetings planned and I appreciate you taking the time to meet me. What I would hope to achieve by our discussion is... '

A smooth transition from small talk to fact-finding is most likely to happen when you are the last person to speak. This requires a little practise and is a good habit to develop in all communications.

Too frequently, what actually happens is: the salesperson introduces himself; the ice-breaker goes on aimlessly; the buyer finally asks a question; the salesperson starts 'selling'; the buyer throws in objections; the salesperson answers the objections; the buyer remains unconvinced; the salesperson goes for the 'close'; the buyer says 'leave it with me'; the sale is lost! (in reality, it was never opened).

Hold your horses

The fact-finding interview is only for the purpose of extracting customer needs. While it is difficult to achieve, refrain from offering solutions or opinions at this meeting. There are three real dangers:

1. Your comments may inspire a follow-up question. You will become the interviewee and find yourself answering instead of asking questions.
2. You could be distracted from the purpose of the meeting which was to *get* information, not to give it.
3. You will dilute the impact of your second visit if the customer already knows the major selling points of your product or service.

How to conduct a professional fact-finding meeting

The type of questions asked at the initial sales interview will vary from customer to customer, though trial and error will indicate the fact-finding most suitable to extract the best information. The questions should follow a pattern and be relevant to the buyer's particular circumstances. A few questions you might consider including are:

- If I could wave a magic wand over the system you are using now, how would you improve it?
- What would you like to be able to do with your new service or equipment that you cannot do now?
- Should you decide to do business with me, what would you expect from me and my company?
- Including some or all of these questions in your fact-finding will help the buyer to focus on his or her particular needs and this information will be invaluable when you return with your proposal.
- Where did I go wrong?

If you have difficulty arranging a further meeting it may be a signal that the fact-finding has not gone well and corrective action may be required. Ask yourself:

- Did I plan the interview properly?
- Did I ask the right questions?
- Did I ask enough of the right questions?
- Did I give away too much information?
- Did I make the buyer feel uncomfortable?
- Did I lose control of the interview?

In practice, if the fact-finding was carried out professionally, the buyer should be eager to meet you again if only because he has no idea what you plan to offer.

WHAT BUYERS WANT YOU TO DO!

Delegates tell me that they find the following mnemonic of great value when trying to remember the importance of fact-finding when approaching decision makers. It is appropriately entitled:

THE CUSTOMERS.
Tell me why you have called
Help me find solutions to my problems
Explore my specific needs

Consider my feelings
Use my time wisely
Show me the proof
Talk my language
Offer realistic proposals
Make me feel important
Empathize with me and my problems
Relax – I will feel uncomfortable otherwise
Skip the small talk – Let's get down to business!

TIMING YOUR PROPOSAL

Once the buyer has agreed to an appointment, it is important to have the opportunity to explain your proposal face-to-face. It is essential that you follow these guidelines:

- Before you leave the customer's office, explain what you are going to do with the information and ask for another appointment.
- Ask how many copies of the proposal he or she requires. This will tell you how many other people may influence the buying decision.
- Send a copy of the proposal or quotation to arrive before your intended visit. Give the buyer enough time to digest the important details thus reducing the risk of hearing: 'I need more time to read through this document.'

The chronology of these events is important. If you send your proposal and then look for an appointment, you may not get one!

TEN KEY POINTS ON FACT-FINDING

- This is the crucial part of the selling process – fail at this stage and you simply will not sell!

- Decide in advance of your visit to make this a one- or two-call close.
- The key part of the fact-finding interview is a clear explanation of what you are hoping to achieve and what you intend to do with the information.
- Remember that only a small number of salespeople carry out this vital part of the sales process correctly. This gives you a major competitive edge.
- Design a personal fact-finding sheet and use it on every call, regardless of how proficient you become.
- Remember that the purpose of the interview is only to get information. The customer may seize upon every comment you make and you will lose control.
- Give as little information as is reasonable at this first meeting. Resist the temptation to sell.
- Write down the important details of your opening statement. Edit and practise it until you feel comfortable.
- Have some information about your customer and ensure that you get all the personal details right.
- Remember, good fact-finding prevents sloppy selling.

Next chapter

In Chapter 7 we will discuss the proposal in some detail. Prior to that please use the fact-finding sheets (Figure 6.1) and the interview preparation checklist (Figure 6.2) to plan your calls. When you become used to them, take whatever ideas you can use and personalize your own fact-finder. You will be pleasantly surprised what it will do for your confidence at the sales interview and, more importantly, buyer attitudes.

7

Creating Winning Proposals

When you submit your proposal to the customer you have already completed 90 per cent of the work but this is the 10 per cent you will get paid for. Your ability to create winning proposals will not only significantly improve your hit rates but also dramatically increase your opportunity to earn. In this crucial chapter we will concentrate on the following:

- gaining the motivation to produce outstanding sales proposals
- developing the skills that will enable you to produce them.

See pages 129-31 for examples of winning proposals (Figure 7.1).

GAINING THE MOTIVATION TO PRODUCE OUTSTANDING SALES PROPOSALS

It is a lot of work so why bother?

There are several compelling reasons why it is in your interests to produce outstanding proposals:

- All professional buyers have to justify the purchase, to spend company money without a written commitment from the supplier would have serious repercussions.
- In competitive markets, there is every chance that your rivals are already producing proposals – you have got to go one better.
- If the standard of proposal in your industry is mediocre, this gives you an outstanding opportunity.
- As we all know, it can be difficult to unseat a rival company who have had the business for years. However, when your set of documents are compared against the 'efforts' of the people who actually have the business, it may cause the buyer to have a major rethink.

This is where the 'little people' have a big advantage over the major companies. Just because you are small, it does not mean that you cannot produce a little 'magic' and create an outstanding set of documents.

What is a proposal?

When you submit a proposal to a customer this is what you are saying: I fully understand what the problem is; and I am capable of delivering the solution.

If you cannot produce a document that satisfies these two fundamentals, there is a real chance that you will not get the business – regardless of how much effort that goes into its production.

To bid or not to bid?

One of the most difficult words for a salesperson to utter is 'no'. Because we are so indoctrinated in achieving sales, every request for a proposal alerts us to produce a time-consuming document on the basis of 'I have nothing to lose'. One of the first decisions you have to make is, are you going to bid for the business – or are you not?

- Is it worthwhile and profitable?
- Are you capable of doing it?
- Is there a real chance of getting the business?
- Will it impact the service you give to others?

If the answer is 'no' then don't waste any more time. Explain your reasons to the buyer, thank him or her for their interest and devote your time to something more profitable.

If you decide to compete for the business!

You have to make a decision right now: are you going to submit the best possible set of documents or are you just going to go through the motions? Changes in buying habits, keener competition and consumer demands compel salespeople to chase business with one clear objective and that is to win!

When I started in the sales consultancy business many years ago, I realized that if I was going to make it I would have to be much more professional in my approach than my rivals. I only had one ambition with a proposal and that was to get the business. If I have ever done anything right in my career it was to be totally focused on producing a set of documents that I knew none of my competitors were prepared to match. Once I made a decision that I wanted the business, this is how I went about it:

- I conducted a fact-finding meeting eliciting as much essential information as possible.
- Absolutely no selling took place at these meetings (in fact I would tell them nothing).
- I became totally immersed in writing the proposal.
- I telephoned to clarify important details from the customer.
- I completed the proposal, editing and rewriting where appropriate.
- I then finalized and produced the proposal.

Remember that you don't have to be the biggest, the cheapest or even the best, you have only got to offer the best solution to the customers needs.

HOW TO PRODUCE WINNING PROPOSALS

Obtain an appointment before sending the proposal

This point was covered in the previous chapter but there is no harm in repeating it. The last thing you need is to put a lot of work into your proposal only to have it filed away without as much as a glance. To ensure that this does not happen, get an appointment to meet for the purpose of discussing your solutions *before* you leave the customer's office.

Use non-threatening language when seeking this appointment. You might say:

> What I would like to do is go away and have a think about how best I can satisfy your stated needs. I will put together a discussion document which will outline my understanding of your requirements, and how we would propose to tackle them. I will have completed my work on this by... Would you be available to meet me on...? Customers rarely challenge this.

Send a copy of your proposal to arrive ahead of your meeting

Once you are certain that getting an appointment is not an issue it makes sense to arrange for the buyer to have a copy of the documents a few hours before your visit. This will give him or her the opportunity to digest the main points and take notes for your discussion. Not only will it save valuable time, it also ensures that the buyer's comments are based on some consideration – not a spontaneous reaction.

Covering letters should be personalized

It is difficult to understand why any salesperson would spend time submitting a proposal to a customer and then spoil everything with a poorly thought out standard introductory letter, usually worded as follows:

> Thank you for the courtesy extended to me on my recent visit to your office. I have pleasure in submitting details of our proposal to install our… I thank you for the opportunity to quote and if any further details are required please do not hesitate to contact me!

Whatever happened to the nice friendly rapport that was established at the meeting?

Words like 'recent visit' confirm that it is a standard letter. Clichés such as 'do not hesitate to contact me' are overused and unimaginative, and the onus is also on the customer to respond (contact me).

Make the letter warm and friendly

The reason why many salespeople send standard introductory letters is because they lack what they perceive as letter-writing skills. As all the details are covered in the proposal, it merely requires some reference to the meeting along with a brief explanation of the contents. Remember you are writing a letter to a person you have developed a relationship with and not an anonymous department. Look on the customer as being a 'friendly' business contact and write the letter accordingly.

> It was very good of you to give me so much of your time on Tuesday morning, I enjoyed the discussion with yourself and Sandra.
>
> What I am submitting to you is my understanding of your requirements and how we propose to tackle your most urgent concerns. While I know that both of you have reservations about the costs, I hope you will also be pleasantly surprised with the comparison made with your present system.

> There were other issues of concern and I will look forward to discussing them when I meet you on Friday.

Of course this letter can be greatly improved but at least it's a start!

Where possible use bullet points

An essential aspect of writing proposals is brevity. Enlist the help of others in editing the document down to the minimum amount of words required. Remember that every page represents an opportunity to reinforce your selling message so avoid eclipsing essential points with too much text.

Find out who else (will read) or require a copy

It is important to find out who the MAN is, the person with:

Money
Authority
Need

In many cases this may be three different people. Sending all three of them a highly technical proposal will work against you if only one of the readers understands the document. Simply by asking, 'who else will require a copy of this proposal?' will provide you with all the information you require. Produce a technical document for those who understand the technicalities and a non-technical one for those who do not! So as not to offend them put the technical specifications in with the appendix. Remember, always write in the reader's language.

Personalize every page

We have talked a lot about the importance of personalizing all the information. In order to ensure that the customer is aware that this is not a standard document, where possible draw reference on every page to some information gleaned from your fact-finding. It only has to be a brief mention such as: 'You mentioned...'; 'I know you were concerned...'; or 'Sandra expressed...'

If your summary is accurate and it has the added credibility of support from people who recognize their own comments, your proposal will, at the very least, be taken seriously.

Don't ignore the power of the 'little people'

Frequently you will have important information supplied by staff members who may perceive themselves as unimportant to the overall purchase. Many salespeople ignore the influence these people can have in deciding who wins the order. If you have reason to draw reference to their views or assistance mention it in the proposal – it provides recognition for the role that they played.

Whether you get the business or not, if a member of staff has been of any assistance to you, their morale and motivation will be greatly enhanced by dropping them a brief note of thanks. It is also consistent with the philosophy of 'creating customers', some day the little mousey guy in the corner may become 'king rat!'

Use customers' logos if possible and appropriate

This is an idea I have always found to be successful. I would copy the company's logo from the buyer's business card and have the proposal cover printed at considerable expense. (Today, that process is very inexpensive.) The proposal was then bound and produced in whatever numbers I required.

The bottom line is this. I didn't get all the business that I tendered for – but I got most of it. I apply the same principle to all my documentation to this very day. You may not like the idea, but it worked for me and remember that it is unlikely that you will ever lose an order because you tried to be more professional than the rest!

EXAMPLES OF WINNING PROPOSALS

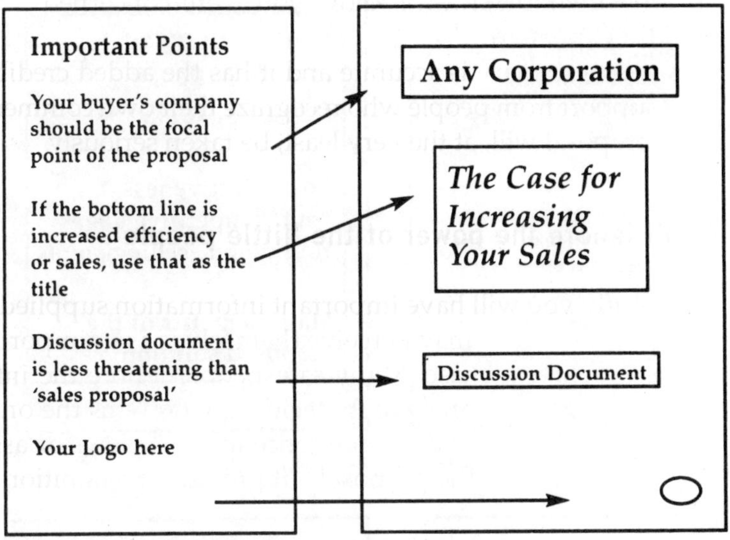

Figure 7.1a *Examples of winning proposals*

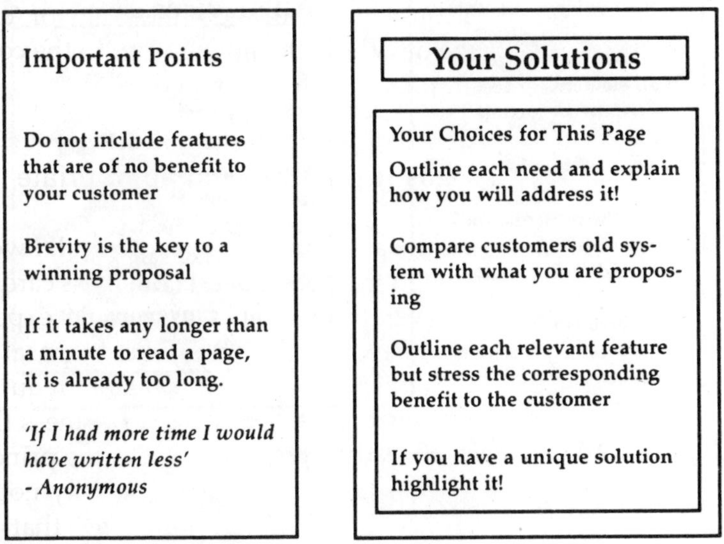

Figure 7.1b *Examples of winning proposals*

Important Points

Whatever essential benefits that were discussed and agreed at the fact-finding stage should be brought to the fore.

If cost is the prime motivation, that should bethe main point and outlined clearly

Prioritize the benefits

The Benefits To The Customer

It will increase...
It will save...
It will solve...

Cost effectiveness
Your competitive edge
Your unique selling points

Major benefits of the proposed solution

Figure 7.1c *Examples of winning proposals*

Important Points

Customers will appreciate a breakdown of all costs

Use your own judgement if all elements of cost are required – include them in your submission

Make the presentation of your costings easy to read and understand

If an item is very technical put a brief explantation in brackets

The Costs

All services...

training
development costs
man day costs
installation and delivery
maintenance
license fees
payment terms
conditions of sale
government taxes
currency conversion rates
total costs

Figure 7.1d *Examples of winning proposals*

Important Points

This is information for your customer that he or she may wish to read – but not an essential part of your overall sales proposal

To avoid lengthy explanations in the main body of your proposal you can draw reference to the appendix at the back

Appendix

You could include...

List of customers
Technical specifications
Product warranty
Company guarantees
Your mission statement
Your company profile
Product brouchers
Samples
Letters from customers
Summary of proposal

Figure 7.1e *Examples of winning proposals*

TEN KEY POINTS ON CREATING WINNING PROPOSALS

- You have already done 90 per cent of the work – this is the 10 per cent you get paid for.
- This is where smaller operators can compete on a par with the big guys.
- Your proposal says 'I understand your problem and this is my solution.'
- You do not have to be the biggest – you only have to offer the best solution.
- Find out who should get a copy of your proposal – endorse names on documents.
- Avoid overused clichés – use your own personal style.
- Try and personalize every page of the proposal.
- Don't ignore the power or influence of those who may appear to be 'little people'

- Use the very best technology available to produce outstanding documents.
- Enlist the support of others to assist you in editing and refining the proposal.

8

Making Professional Sales Presentations

We are a visually-orientated society. We grow up surrounded by the influences of television, advertising, and various other visual stimuli. The proper use of visuals helps the salesperson control the presentation and maintain the customer's attention. They force the salesperson to organize his or her thoughts in an orderly fashion and condense the message into a concise and more understandable story. In this chapter there are five important skills to master:

- how to plan and personalize the presentation
- how to get maximum support from your audience
- how to make a professional sales presentation
- how to use visual aids
- how to carry out a professional sales demonstration to gain maximum sales.

The importance of learning these skills

If you are serious about a long-term career in selling you will have to make important sales presentations to large groups; your colleagues; major accounts; and key buyers.

In the interests of learning efficiency, and to avoid time-consuming repetition of reading, I have grouped together the skills of making presentations to groups and individuals.

While the methods are very different the skills and attitudes are identical.

HOW TO PLAN AND PERSONALIZE THE PRESENTATION

The best way to present a product is to ensure the presentation satisfies the six Ps:

- plan – good presentations do not just happen, they are planned
- pattern – a step-by-step logical sequence which is easy to follow
- power – a combination of enthusiasm, self-confidence and a positive mental attitude
- proof – provide evidence of all claims which exalt the virtues of your product
- pictures – proper use of visuals helps stimulate and maintain the customer's attention
- participation – get customers involved, ask questions, let them handle the product.

Personalize the information whenever possible

With all the technology available to us, it should be very simple to personalize presentations with company logos, photographs and peoples names.

If presenting to a group and using name cards, have them professionally produced. If you can also put the company logo on the name cards rather than your own, it will be appreciated.

Present your ideas in an orderly manner

The difference between a box of coloured glass and a stained glass window is organization. Relate your points in a logical pattern so that people can follow easily.

Anticipate difficulties and consider response

What will you do if somebody insults you, loses their head when arguing their point or attacks you, your company or your product. It may never happen but if it does and you are not prepared you may regret not having prepared.

When I conducted my very first selling seminar, I was most unfortunate to meet the well-balanced delegate – the man with a chip on both shoulders. Eventually his 'that's all right but' response to every positive idea got the better of me. I reacted badly to his attitude which resulted in me having to apologize to him publicly – ironically the session was on human relations.

I realized that if I was to make a career out of developing others I was likely to meet many difficult people and I anticipated the worst things that delegates could say or do. I considered how I would deal with the most negative, bad-humoured, ill-tempered delegates and how I would respond. Interestingly, every one of those situations presented themselves in the coming years and when they happened I knew how I was going to handle them and convert them to win/win situations. Of all the decisions I have made in my career, this was one of my better ones.

Be a mirror of your message

Last summer, the family went for a picnic and I parked my car beside a white van notable because it looked as if it hadn't been cleaned in a month. What intrigued me was the legend on the side of the van: 'XYZ cleaners – specialists in retail store hygiene'!

An associate told me the story of how a salesperson called to sell him a portable overhead projector and vainly tried to describe it in a series of body movements and hand gestures.

If its uniqueness was its portability, why didn't he bring it with him? Remember you are the message, if you are selling professionalism then you must be professionalism personified.

Maintain a sense of humour but take your role seriously

A sense of humour is an important ingredient in great salespeople and presenters, however, in communicating with groups it is difficult to be funny without offending someone. Selling is a serious business and while a light-hearted backdrop is always welcome – few people will take a clown seriously. It is acceptable to tell of an amusing experience but only if you can relate it well and that no person or group is the target of ridicule, and the story has direct relevance to the topic under discussion.

A few years ago at a sales meeting in Denmark one of the members of my group told a funny story over lunch and the target was a much-maligned minority group. The Chief Executive was not impressed – his wife was a member of that community.

Use the KISS method

Avoid eclipsing the main point of your message by over-communicating. The KISS method means Keep It Short and Sweet or if you prefer, Keep It Simple Stupid!

HOW TO GET MAXIMUM SUPPORT FROM YOUR AUDIENCE

Lap-tops, high-tech projectors and the never-ending stream of new technology practically forces us into higher levels of presentation excellence. Countless sellers already use video conferencing to communicate around the world and who knows what the future has in store? Whatever method you use I strongly urge you to apply all of the following skills.

Explain the audience's role – questions and participation

Generally speaking, audiences are extremely polite and will allow you to run the presentation your way. Unless you tell them, they will be unsure if they should ask questions as you go along or wait until you have finished.

When seeking involvement – start with positive people

In the majority of cases, successive speakers will continue the theme of the opening remarks from your audience. If somebody starts with a negative point, the chances are that the comments will be supported by speaker after speaker and any chance you have of achieving your objective disappears completely.

By selecting those you consider most likely to make positive observation, there is some chance that a positive theme may be maintained.

Stimulate your audience

If you were trying to arouse a member of the opposite sex, what part of their anatomy would you concentrate on? Before you continue, think about your answer for a moment or two and write it down.

Whenever I ask salespeople this question I receive some interesting responses – most of which are wrong. It is of course the brain! A good presentation will stimulate people by asking well thought out questions, showing interest in their interests and seeking their views and opinions.

Tune into WIIFM for better reception

When outlining the objectives for your presentation, you must answer the unasked question from your audience 'what's in it for me?' (WIIFM). Ideas of no personal interest to the listener will fall on deaf ears. Phrase your talk to highlight the interest of the listener.

Use the Nine o'Clock News method

There are few people earning their living by communication who would disagree with the basics of getting your message across: tell them what you are going to tell them; tell them!; then tell them what you have told them!

Use bullet points and expand on them

One of the worst presentations I have ever witnessed came from a 'key' speaker at a conference. He produced black and white overhead transparencies with paragraphs of information which he read word for word. Before long people started drifting away from the seminar and it was the last presentation he delivered to that group.

Bullet points help people to focus on the main message and allow you to add supporting information without distracting the audience away from the main issue.

Use a pleasant tone of voice

Try to develop a good speaking voice so that people will want to listen. Appealing articulation: is pleasant in tone; is natural; has enthusiasm; contains variety; and has volume and clarity.

Good presenters never doubt their ability to add value to any situation be it through force of personality, enthusiasm or their distinct personality and style.

Make it persuasive

In the words of the Greek philosopher Aristotle, in order for people to change views or firmly held beliefs they must be exposed to the three indispensable pillars of persuasion: facts, emotion and credibility.

- Fact – they need a rational appeal to logically justify the new belief. The information supplied must be truthful and stand up to logical examination.
- Emotion – to draw people to your cause they must become motivated emotionally.
- Credibility – they must have sincere belief in the source of the information. To persuade you must be manifestly knowledgeable and of the highest integrity.

Tell it like it is

An airline covered up the crash of an expensive aeroplane and the deaths of three people by listing the crash in its annual report as the 'involuntary conversion of a 747'. The meaning was clear to lawyers but not to most lay people.

Most of us would prefer to be made redundant than to be 'fired' and perhaps it is less painful to 'pass away' rather than die. It is quite acceptable to put a better face on a bad situation – provided everybody understands what you mean. If the answer to a customer request is 'no' make sure that however diplomatically you say it, no-one's time is wasted with false hopes when the answer was always going to be 'no'.

HOW TO MAKE A PROFESSIONAL SALES PRESENTATION

If you begin your presentation well and something goes wrong later, you have some chance to put it right. If you start badly it is extremely difficult to recover.

Every word you utter in your opening remarks will have enormous impact on your audience and it will set the scene for a positive or negative audience reaction to the rest of your presentation.

If you are given 30 minutes to make a presentation, it is a good idea to prepare your material to last about 45 minutes and plan an appropriate place to include it if you run into trouble. Similarly, decide in advance what material is least important if you have to cut it short. In making presentations, apply 'Murphy's Law': anything that can go wrong, will go wrong – at the worst possible moment.

I recall one of the first and most important group presentations of my career. I was competing against all my highly professional rivals and this order meant so much in terms of prestige and company revenue. I became very agitated about this meeting that not surprisingly I was very apprehensive. I spent many hours preparing special personalized slides and rehearsed the presentation with my colleagues several times.

I arrived for the presentation expecting to meet six pleasant, friendly people but was informed that they had invited 25 other managers to attend. On entering the meeting room my colleague tripped over the mat and the box of slides scattered around the floor. When I switched on the projector the bulb blew, then turned to sit on a chair which promptly collapse. As I fell I pulled down all the slides that had just been picked off the floor. The tension in that room while we waited for a replacement bulb was very unsettling. I struggled to get even the slightest spark from an audience who had already seen seven other presentations before I arrived – they were bored. The atmosphere made me more nervous than I have ever been. I delivered the material as well as the situation allowed and only began to relax when it came to questions.

A few days later, to my surprise and delight, I was informed that we had won the contract. When the chief executive introduced me to his sales managers, I listened with embarrassment as he outlined all of the things that went wrong at my presentation: the slides, the bulb, the chair, the slides again, how tense I was and how unsympathetic people were to the comedy of errors that accompanied my performance.

He said the reason he had given me the business was because none of the other presenters had worked as hard on the preparation as I had and I was the only one who seemed to have any understanding of what they were trying to achieve. This incident proved to me that buyers will forgive you for some things provided you overcome these handicaps with outstanding preparation.

Avoid starting with an apology

Recently, I was introduced to a group of business people as their speaker for the day. My host's opening remarks were: 'First of all, to those of you who were here on time, I want to apologize for our late start...'

This is how to blow a presentation in twenty words. I use this as an example because although it may sound courteous by apologizing to those who were on time, it is also humiliating for those who were not. Because the latecomers were uncomfortable about his remarks they became agitated and this added to the tension. In those circumstances I had to call on all my skills to get the presentation under control.

Controlling nerves

Many people confuse an incompetent speaker with a nervous one. These are the traits of an incompetent presenter: poor personal appearance; weak voice projection; fumbling around with slides, etc; lack of eye contact with the audience; beginning with an apology; talking about himself or herself; saying things such as: 'I'm not very good at making presentations'; speaking too fast or too slowly; projecting an unfriendly or cold facial expression.

Long before the miracle of television, political observers wrote constantly of Abraham Lincoln's 'podium nerves'. A nervous speaker may suffer personally for a few minutes, but with an incompetent speaker, the audience suffers.

If you are nervous about presenting, then you are in good company. The late Richard Burton claimed he was physically ill before every performance and in a poll of human fears, twice as many people were more afraid of speaking in public than they were of dying! Consider these very important tips on controlling nerves.

- We are all human and vulnerable. If you are trying your best, people will tend to be very sympathetic.
- As most people in your audience do not see themselves as great presenters, they will be reluctant to be overly critical if you slip up here and there.
- The best antidote to fear is total organization.
- Rehearse repeatedly your introductory statement. It may only last 30 seconds but being able to do it without faltering will do much for your confidence.
- If you are particularly concerned about controlling nerves, produce an introductory slide or overhead. As you open the presentation switch on the projector and you will find that peoples eyes will immediately move to the screen. That will give you a moment or two to relax.
- Another very good way to relax is to prepare a question consistent with your presentation that you can put to your audience for response. This early interaction can do great things to settle nerves. Make certain that the question is relevant and that it ties in with what you are doing.
- Prepare yourself for every eventuality. What if they are hostile, what if they don't wish to participate?
- Involve the audience as quickly as possible.
- Use good eye contact with your audience: this is the best way to convey confidence and reduce personal tension.
- Smile warmly and try to convey a welcome to your audience.
- Dismiss all negative thoughts about yourself. Visualize yourself doing a good job.

- Use your own words, your own style and be yourself. Do whatever it is that makes you comfortable.
- When you stand up in front of a group of people, they don't know how much or how little experience you have of presenting – this works to your advantage.
- The only person who knows you are nervous is you.
- If you prepare well, within two minutes your fears and nerves will subside.

When I was offered my first job as a sales manager, I very nearly turned it down because part of the role involved speaking to groups of 50 or 60 people. It is ironic that today, this is how I make my living. I still get butterflies before presentations but now I can control my nerves – they do not control me.

Give out notes after the presentation

Never hand out notes before your presentation unless it is essential. If you do, this is what will happen: when you are talking, some people will be reading and this is very distracting for presenters; you may be discussing page 2 but others are reading page 5; they will know what you are about to say – thus totally undermining your reason for being there.

As the presenter you are responsible for establishing the atmosphere You have a greater chance of achieving this if you keep people focused on the same subject at the same time.

The importance of visuals

When relying on the spoken word alone for communication it is important to remember that:

- an estimated 90 per cent of a message is misinterpreted or forgotten completely

- we retain only 10 per cent of what we hear
- adding appropriate visual aids to the spoken word increases retention to approximately 50 per cent.

Here are some examples of the various types of sales material a salesperson could use: testimonials from other customers; newspaper reviews, articles or cuttings; photographs; maps; product components; mock-ups; films; facts and figures; artists' impressions; and cartoons.

In directory advertising, salespeople will frequently use a visual of what the customer's advertisement will look like and this rarely fails to generate a discussion. I also know an insurance salesperson who uses his artistic talents to age a photograph of a prospective client to highlight the need for planning for retirement. I personally would not use this idea but it works very well for him. With evidence such as this, why do most salespeople rely so heavily on verbal persuasion, aided only by standard quotations? It is more difficult to make a sale solely on the basis of a conversation than it will ever be if your comments are backed up by visual aids.

Tell it with enthusiasm

The following story illustrates how an enthusiastic approach can be a recipe for success.

In the early 1960s a cigarette was launched on the British market. It was supported by a powerful advertising campaign and no expense was spared in getting the message to the public. The scene was of a party with happy people dancing to the music of the day – except for one forlorn figure in the corner, looking very sad and depressed. Not having much luck at the party he leaves and heads for a deserted promenade. As he stands dejectedly under a street lamp he takes out a cigarette and lights up. A hypnotic voice says 'You're never alone with a Strand.'

The advertising campaign was probably one of the most spectacular failures of all time as it hardly sold a cigarette.

The subliminal message that people were receiving was 'if you have bad breath, body odour, acne and dandruff these are the cigarettes for you'!

The tobacco company changed to another agency. They took the same cigarette, put it in a different box and gave it a new name. They advertised it using a similar party scene but on this occasion everyone was having fun, with happy faces and enthusiastic figures reaching for the new product. The company called the cigarette 'Embassy' and it became the most successful cigarette in British tobacco history. Remember – enthusiasm sells.

Watch your body language

Audiences tend to react to visual signals over the verbal signals. If you are stiff, sombre and uncomfortable your message will also be seen in a negative light. Set aside a period of time every day to study the body language of others. At the same time, be aware of your own body talk. When making presentations: watch out for spontaneous physical reactions; try to work out what signals you are receiving; observe gestures, postures and expressions; check if the signals are consistent or contrary to what is being said.

It is obviously important to be able to judge how your audience is reacting to your talk. Understanding body language gives you the advantage of adjusting your presentation accordingly.

Summary on making sales presentations

- prepare well in advance
- the first 30 seconds are critical
- avoid having to start with an apology
- use the Nine o'Clock News method
- use bullet points and expand on them
- personalize the information whenever possible

- explain the audience's role – questions and participation
- hand out notes *after* the presentation
- when seeking involvement – start with positive people
- anticipate objections and rehearse response
- if you have something unique – highlight it
- maintain a sense of humour but take your role seriously
- use a pleasant tone of voice
- tune into WIIFM for better reception
- make it persuasive
- tell it with enthusiasm
- present your ideas in an orderly manner
- use the KISS method
- stimulate your audience
- be a mirror of your message
- watch your body language
- tell it like it is
- use the six Ps to better presentations

HOW TO USE VISUAL AIDS

Consider these important points:

- Arrange your visuals before you meet the customer. Fumbling around will distract the customer's attention.
- No matter how many times you have told a story or shown a particular visual, the customer is hearing it for the first time, so be enthusiastic.
- Keep your visuals clean. A shabby visual will communicate all the wrong messages and it is blatantly unprofessional.
- Become totally familiar with your visuals. In many cases you may have to demonstrate them wrong way up.
- Avoid showing two pages at the same time. If you are demonstrating a point from an open folder, cover one of the pages with a plain white sheet of paper. This ensures the customer is focusing on the factors you consider vital.

- Do not allow the customer to handle your folder, because by doing so, you have lost control. In the unavoidable event of it happening, stop talking and redirect the customer back to a point that you wish to make. At the same time politely take back the folder.
- Do not read. Use different words to make your point. This will help to reinforce the point.
- Personalize whenever possible and show only what is required. Your presentation will be greatly improved if you tailor your words to convey that you are showing these visuals because they apply to the customer's situation.
- Verify understanding. Do not continue unless the customer has completely understood. A good, snappy presentation will maintain his or her interest. There is nothing to be gained by emphasizing a point the customer has grasped already.

Properly used, the presentation is a powerful persuader. It provides the opportunity of eliminating objections before they arise.

HOW TO CARRY OUT A PROFESSIONAL SALES DEMONSTRATION TO GAIN MAXIMUM SALES

Demonstrating a product is an art in itself. Here are the essentials.

Don't bore the buyer with marathon demonstrations

There are two very different demonstrations we need to give to a prospective buyer: a sales demonstration and an operational demonstration. They should not be given together.

- A *sales* demonstration is given to show how the product will solve the customer's specific problems and this should only take place after the fact-finding stage is complete.

- An *operational* demonstration only takes place when the customer has made the purchase or has taken delivery of the product.

Understanding this concept is critical to increasing your hit rates from presentations to sales orders. A most important consideration for a customer who wants to buy a copier is the quality of the prints. How to clear a 'paper jam' is only a consideration when the machine has been installed.

Not so long ago, I worked with a team of copier salespeople and the plan was to observe their presentation and demonstrating skills. In every case they demonstrated the copier to senior people who were also the buyers. These are some of my observations:

- each demonstration took an average of 38 minutes (the longest was 73 minutes)
- everybody fell into the trap of boring the buyer with sales and operational demonstrations
- none of the 15 salespeople ever mentioned a benefit. They couldn't because they didn't ask any fact-finding questions
- introducing the 'operational' dimension caused all kinds of problems with paper jams, print registration and a host of other weaknesses.

Rather ironically, we agreed that none of the prospective buyers was ever likely to use the copiers themselves – so why did they need a demonstration on how to clear a paper jam? Even if they were the operators, the presentation stage was not the time to explain operational methods. At that point, this sales team had a hit rate of one in every 16 demonstrations; subsequently they improved this to one in four by doing the following:

- fact-finding the customers needs before the demonstration
- resisting the temptation to show all the product features and concentrating only on those aspects that were relevant to the customer

- giving only a 'sales' demonstration, which brought the average demonstration time down to 12 minutes
- selling what the product could do and not the product itself.

If you have to demonstrate your product occasionally, reminding yourself of these points will help increase your hit rates.

Eliminate technical jargon completely

If you really want to embarrass buyers just use words that they cannot understand. The use of jargon and buzz words does not impress the customer – it confuses them.

Make the most of every minute

Genuine buyers are busy people. Show respect for their time and they will return the compliment. Beware of people who have all day to talk to you – our selling experience is that they talk to everybody and buy nothing.

Open with problem-seeking questions

When demonstrating a product it is more efficient to show only what needs to be shown. A couple of well thought-out questions will give you all the information you need. For example: 'What would you like to be able to do with your new product that you cannot do now?'

For more information on problem seeking questions see fact-finding in Chapter 6.

Never highlight your product's weaknesses – emphasize strengths

I find it remarkable to note the number of salespeople who go out of their way to say what the product cannot do, such as: 'This is not as fast as our other model'; or 'What you will not be able to do is...'

In one demonstration I observed a buyer incorrectly load paper into a laser printer and it subsequently became snagged. The salesperson referred to it as a 'paper jam' when a more complimentary description was a 'misfeed'. It was not a weakness of the machine but the way the paper was loaded yet the customer perceived it as technical deficiency and didn't buy!

Sell the difference

If a customer is already using one of your older models or a piece of competitive equipment, he or she will be most impressed if you can demonstrate the difference between the piece of equipment you are trying to sell and their existing equipment. It will also do a lot for your credibility as an expert in your profession.

Treat your product with respect

Customers will not be impressed with salespeople who don't think enough of their products to keep them clean and in very good demonstration order. Some time ago, I went to a store to buy a personal computer. As the salesperson was demonstrating a PC, he accidentally kicked a monitor that was sitting on the floor behind him. I was concerned that he may have damaged it but he replied: 'It's OK, it is only a customer's monitor that's here for a service'!

I doubt if he realized that his comments and his total disregard for his product and customers caused him to lose not only a sale – but a prospective buyer forever?

Remember to sell benefits – not features

This point is already covered in Chapter 4 but no harm to have a brief reminder. For example, a remote control with a high-tech projector is only a *feature* of the product, one of its *benefits* is that it improves presentation excellence.

Avoid unrealistic and unnecessary guarantees

The time when salespeople mention guarantees is usually when talking about or demonstrating the product. If you must mention a guarantee explain precisely what you mean. Failure to do so can cost you more than a sale.

Guarantees are a sensitive area with many experienced buyers who quite correctly feel let down when the guarantee turns out to be not a guarantee. Failure to explain guarantees correctly can: destroy your own personal credibility; cause a lot of unnecessary customer service problems later on; and cost you the sale!

I once accompanied a sales manager to a major sales call and at the appropriate time he said: 'We guarantee a four-hour response time to service calls.' The customer replied: 'What happens if it's five hours?' To which the sales manager responded: 'I am the sales manager and if you have a problem you contact me and I will put it right!'

That comment cost him a sale and very nearly the entire account. The customer responded angrily: 'How can you guarantee me four-hour service and then accept that it could be five? In fact the last service call I put in was not responded to for two days.'

Recently, I watched an advertisement on television in which a courier company guaranteed delivery of a package to New York by 10 am the next day. I haven't looked into it but I am certain that the guarantee does not and cannot mean what it promises. What happens if the courier has an accident? What about fog at the airport at either end? What about a crash? I believe, as a professional sales trainer, that this type of advertising is deceitful and blatantly unprofessional. What they probably mean is that they will refund your money if the package is not delivered on time, which is not the same as what they guarantee. Tell the customer exactly what you mean and they will appreciate it!

Empathize every time – all the time

Try and see the selling process from the customer's point of view. Remember, you don't have to agree – you only have to understand.

SUMMARY ON MAKING SALES DEMONSTRATIONS

- don't bore the buyer with marathon demonstrations
- eliminate technical jargon completely
- make the most of every minute
- open with problem-seeking questions
- never highlight your product's weaknesses
- sell the difference
- treat the customer and product with respect
- remember to sell benefits – not features
- avoid unrealistic guarantees
- talk with enthusiasm
- empathize every time.

TEN KEY POINTS ON MAKING PROFESSIONAL SALES PRESENTATIONS

- Remember the six Ps – plan, pattern, power, proof, pictures and participation.
- Never use equipment or materials inferior in standard to audience expectation.

- Avoid ever having to start with an apology – this will totally unsettle you.
- Remember: the first 30 seconds of your presentation are critical.
- Use bullet points to highlight main points and expand on them verbally.
- When seeking participation – start with positive people.
- Use the Nine o'Clock News method to reinforce essential messages.
- Remember the pillars of persuasion: facts, emotion and credibility.
- Tune into WIIFM, in other words 'what's in it for me'.
- Hand out your notes – after the presentation.

9

Negotiating Profitable Sales

As we all know, the only way a salesperson's performance can be measured is by the consistent production of orders. While it is true to say that many sales are lost long before the presentation is concluded, failure to tie up the paperwork or sell at a profit means that all your efforts have been in vain.

In this chapter we will discuss:

- how to create the conditions which inspire people to buy
- how to handle customer concerns about buying
- how to use negotiating skills to increase buyer satisfaction
- how to build customer confidence on price
- how to plan the negotiation
- how to use negotiating skills to increase sales and profits.

HOW TO CREATE THE CONDITIONS THAT INSPIRE PEOPLE TO BUY

Before you even consider asking a customer for business, there must be mutual agreement on two important points. First, it has been confirmed that a need actually exists (this should be evident from your fact-finding); and second, it is acknowledged that your product or service can fulfil that need.

Any attempt to secure the business without these two conditions, is unprofessional, unethical and a total waste of good selling time.

Helping the buyer to buy

Making the buying decision will be easier for the customer if he or she is convinced that:

- You are a professional; you represent a professional organization and everything you have told the customer is truthful and above reproach.
- The product or service you are selling has a successful track record and it will do all the things for the customer that you promised it would do.
- The customer completely understands what he or she is receiving for his or her money and, just as importantly, understands what he or she is not getting.
- The customer must be confident that, in the event of any post-sale problems, you and your company will honour your commitments without any further investment of time or money on the customer's part.
- All questions have been answered to the customer's total satisfaction and there are no other problems which should stop him or her from buying except the decision itself.

Points to remember at the closing stages

The salesperson who can, through a creative presentation, eliminate most of the customer's fears before asking for the order is most likely to have more successful experiences. Building these crucial points into your selling style will help eliminate some of the reasons for failure.

Be professional. No matter how great the temptation, never beg the customer to buy. On the rare occasion that this method succeeds, you lose credibility and any prospects for repeat business.
Expect to win the business. Customers are unconsciously affected by your attitude. Radiate confidence, by your manner, posture and voice, that a decision to grant you the order is a safe one.
Be polite and pleasant. An aggressive or presumptuous manner suits few and is offensive to most. At the same time it is imperative that you demonstrate a quiet calmness that dispels any idea that survival depends on getting an order or a unique experience.
Avoid sidetracking. Never introduce something into the closing stages which has not been discussed earlier. This will divert the customer's attention away from what is a most critical part of the presentation.
Buying is a serious business. While a little humour is to be encouraged, beware of clowning around at the closing stage; the danger is that the entire presentation becomes a joke and it will be difficult to return to serious business.
Be positive. Avoid questions that invite a negative response, for example: 'You would not care to have it, would you?'; or 'I suppose you would not be interested.' This approach will not inspire the customer to buy.
Don't forget the 'carrot'. Inevitably, there will always be people who need further encouragement to buy. Many experienced salespeople try to have some little 'extra' in reserve, to give that additional motivation to the buyer to act now!

Asking for the business

First time stories are best and no sales presentation will sound as good the second time around. Tying up the business when all the benefits are fresh in the buyer's mind is obviously important so this is the best time to look for a positive commitment. When you complete your presentation one of five circumstances will prevail:

1. If you have approached the sales presentation in the recommended manner there is an excellent chance that you will be offered the business (this is the experience of the majority).
2. Your buyer will have concerns or problems regarding the purchase. These must be addressed to his or her satisfaction before any further business can be concluded. Any attempt to secure the order before these issues are resolved will be met with resistance. (See pages 158-9 'Handling customer concerns about the purchase')
3. You will not be offered the business, but you are getting good buying signals (see next point) so just ask for the order – contrary to popular belief there are no magic phrases. Here are some examples: 'If you are happy with our discussion, I would like to have your business'; 'If you give me an order today I can have it installed for you by the weekend'; 'If you are happy to go ahead, I promise to take personal responsibility in ensuring that all our commitments are honoured within 24 hours'; 'On the basis of our discussions, I am satisfied that this proposal is the most practical, cost-effective solution to your (problem) – if you are also satisfied, may I write up your order?' These are only suggestions and I recommend that you use any closing statement that you are comfortable about using.
4. The buyer does not give you the business but may pay you a great courtesy and explain why. How you deal with this is personal choice. If you concede the business, be gracious, thank the customer and leave the door open for future sales calls.
5. Unless you are clairvoyant, the most difficult of all: when the buyer takes refuge in 'I need time to think about this.' It may be a diplomatic way of telling you that you are not going to get the order, or it may be genuine – in both cases asking for the order is redundant.

I trust you will agree that there is only one scenario out of the five where asking for the order is appropriate. So where does 'never give up asking' fit into common sense selling?

Buying signals

Buying signals will come from any one of a combination of body language, questions or comments. If the customer picks up the product, measures it or keeps returning to inspect a particular feature, this at least indicates a high level of interest. Questions such as: 'When can you deliver?'; 'What discount will you give me?'; or 'What is the warranty period?' suggest that the customer is in a buying frame of mind and it is appropriate to maintain the discussion in the same positive light. Each of these questions, if handled correctly, could result in concluding the business. For example:

Customer: 'When can you deliver?'
Salesperson: 'How soon do you want it?'
Customer: 'I would need it by Friday'
Salesperson: 'If we can tie up the paperwork now, I will give you personal assurance that it will arrive by noon on Friday. Is that OK with you?'

HOW TO HANDLE CUSTOMER CONCERNS ABOUT BUYING

I refuse to call this 'overcoming objections' (standard sales training description) because its very title implies a competition or a 'showdown' between the buyer and the salesperson. For professional salespeople this is a time of excitement – not a battle of wits or a competition to see who is the smarter!

In my lifetime I have seen salespeople lose countless sales, not because the buyer threw out a difficult question but because the salesperson responded in ways such as:

- Totally over-reacting (taking negative remarks about the product personally). A salesperson who embarrasses a customer simply will not sell!
- Pouncing back with a smart reply. Buyers do not appreciate a programmed response straight from the last sales training session.
- Trying to compete with the customer's opinion. No matter how ill-informed a buyer may be, avoid upstaging him or her with your superior knowledge. Do it gently and show consideration for his or her feelings.
- Becoming agitated or aggressive. Customers are obviously influenced by the salesperson's attitude – aggression will be met with aggression followed by another lost sale!

A genuine customer concern, properly handled, is a milestone towards the sale, not a brick wall with 'no sale' written across it.

I need time to think about this

One of the most difficult statements to overcome is: 'I want to think it over', simply because one doesn't know if it is genuine or false. Even a combination of skill and experience won't always guarantee a successful outcome. However here are some suggestions that might help: 'While I would like to have your business, it is absolutely essential that you are also completely happy with the purchase. May I ask you what it is that concerns you?'

If the buyer has a genuine concern, he or she will tell you, in which case you should attempt to reassure. If it sounds insincere – it probably is – in which case your time might be better invested in a graceful departure. Remember, you cannot win them all but that should never dissuade you from trying!

Prepare for the worst

You should rarely encounter any level of customer resistance that you have not thought through many times beforehand. Put yourself in the customer's place and try to imagine all the reasons why somebody would object to buying your product or service. Consider all the possible points against, and all those in favour. When customers in a live situation raise these same comments you will respond in a more relaxed frame of mind.

The positive side to customer resistance

Buyers come in all shapes, sizes and attitudes. Some communicate their concerns politely, others aggressively while others may even sound rude. How we respond will, to some extent, dictate our level of success in achieving sales. When customers object, console yourself in the knowledge that:

- an order obtained without an element of customer resistance is extremely rare
- negative comments will occur at any time during a presentation. Frequently, they indicate that the customer is interested but requires reassurance on a number of points
- some buyers will prefer not to show their hand until all the negatives are eliminated
- generally speaking, the customer who has no questions to ask has no desire to buy either.

Some points on handling customer concerns

No attempt is made here to review every possible reason as to why a customer may be concerned about the purchase. The intent is to focus on some of the most common causes of sales resistance and, having created awareness, eliminate as many as possible. The following are six important points in handling customer concerns:

1. Listen carefully
2. Remain calm
3. Never interrupt
4. Restate the concern or question.
5. Speak in a reassuring manner.
6. Empathize with the customer when responding.

Analysing the consistency of customer remarks

One of the most beneficial exercises that you can carry out as a salesperson is to write down the consistency of customer statements, remarks, objections or reasons for not buying. This will provide you with valuable information that you can use for self-analysis and ultimately self-improvement. Let us take a few of the most common.

'I want to think about it.' Customers will not always tell you the real reason why they have chosen not to buy from you (and why should they?) If it is the most frequent objection you hear it may be that: you are pressurizing buyers into a decision; you are closing sales before you open them; or your presentation is turning people off.

While it is impossible to speculate (without personal information) on what may cause a buyer to say 'I want to think it over' one thing is certain, if you look deeply at your selling style you will probably find the answer.

'You are much too expensive.' Why would one salesperson in a small sales team encounter price as a major objection – while all of the others, selling the same product in the same market have no problem at all? The finger of suspicion points at the salesperson. Perhaps the problem is: no belief in your product; poor fact-finding resulting in lack of customer desire to buy; poor presentation of the product benefits; and customers not wishing to buy from the salesperson.

'You are a great salesperson.' This is not a compliment, it is an insult – especially when the customer does not buy! What the buyer is saying is that you represent all of their perceptions of the typical salesperson. You are friendly but pushy and probably persecuted him for an order. The only way to

get rid of you is to boost your ego rather than tell you what they really think.

If you have been receiving this 'compliment' from buyers, I imagine that by this stage you have already worked out where you are going wrong.

Finally, talk to your colleagues at work, ask them to relate the consistency of the objections that they hear in their everyday selling role. If you receive comments that they do not, you can be sure that it points to a weakness in your personal sales presentation.

HOW TO USE NEGOTIATING SKILLS TO INCREASE BUYER SATISFACTION

One of the fundamental aspects of negotiating is the ability to get along with others. People who understand the principles of win/win will approach the issue with confidence while others may see it as another hurdle on the way to a sale.

Negotiating can be fun. While buying is a serious business, many customers admit that they thoroughly enjoy this stage of the selling/buying process. In many cases the salesperson has already won the business, it is now just a question of getting the best price.

Don't look on the buyer as your opponent. Try to see the negotiation from both sides of the table: you are trying to help the customer to buy at terms acceptable to him or her but also ensuring a profit for your company.

The buyer's viewpoint. It is the buyer's duty to get the very best deal for his or her company. They want your bottom line and they will use their considerable skills to find out what that line is!

Your viewpoint. You are at a serious disadvantage – because you *think* you are. In reality you have as much going for you as the customer and possibly more, as we shall discover.

HOW TO BUILD CUSTOMER CONFIDENCE ON PRICE

Before we talk about price, consider the following question: if given a choice, would you want to sell the most expensive product in the market or the least expensive?

Hopefully, your answer is 'the most expensive'. Practically all salespeople will make the same decision and why? Most expensive implies superior quality. All our experience indicates that it is more difficult to sell the cheapest product in any range of products because of the perception that their must be something inferior about the product.

Cheap versus expensive

If you pay over the odds for a top-quality product, the worst that can happen is that you lose a little money. If, on the other hand, (in an attempt to save money) you buy a cheaper product and subsequently discover that it will not do the job, it may turn out to be the most expensive purchase you have ever made! Nothing is cheap or inexpensive if it is not capable of doing the job it is required to do!

Do you think your product is too expensive?

Your attitude to price is important. If you believe your product is even a little expensive, you will subconsciously influence the customer to think in the same way. This lack of conviction will manifest itself in offering unwarranted discounts and erosion of profit margins. If you must give a discount, never do so because you think it is overpriced.

Similarly, just because your rivals sell a less expensive product closely resembling your own, or they have decreased their prices, this does not mean that your product is no longer excellent value. There are usually many good reasons why people drop their prices and a little commercial detective work may provide the answers.

Here are some statements frequently put by salespeople concerning price:

- 'in (our) highly competitive market it is all about price'
- 'if you ever get to the stage where you truly believe that price is *the* deciding factor, it is time to have a long hard look at yourself. If it is only about price why would your company want to employ you – surely it would be less expensive to send out a price list?'
- 'are the cheapest products in *your* market-place the biggest sellers?'
- 'is the cheapest car on the road the most popular?'

Compared with the opposition we are too expensive

It is not unusual for competing salespeople to sell practically identical products but with different price tags. Because your rivals have decided to undercut your price, that does not automatically dilute the value of your product. This is where a knowledge of your competitors' strengths and weaknesses, your USPs and professional fact-finding will help tip the scales in your favour. Think of all the benefits you can offer that others can not and highlight those differences to the customer.

How to turn a selling opportunity into a serious default

When a buyer outlines a concern, it may be expressed as: 'It is very expensive'; 'You're 10 per cent more expensive than your nearest rival'; or 'How am I supposed to justify this extra 10 per cent?'

What these typical customer remarks have in common is that they are not objections. The first is a statement, the second an observation and the third is a question. Admittedly, to salespeople who are paranoid about customer comments, they may sound like objections, so they are answered as objections and so they will become objections.

Qualify 'too expensive'

When the customer says the product is 'too expensive', qualify exactly what he or she means by that. It can mean any one of a number of things, maybe it is 'too expensive' in relation to: a comparison with what the customer paid before; what your competitors are charging; what the other quotations are coming in at; what he or she believes it should cost; the amount of money the buyer has available; the perceived value compared against the price.

Failure to qualify what the buyer means will result in you answering the wrong question. For example, not having sufficient funds to purchase is quite different to a belief that the product is not worth the money.

Bear in mind that price in many cases is a smokescreen for the underlying concern and only through qualifying these concerns can you discover whether it is sincere or false.

Bridging the gap with benefits

When a customer compares your price unfavourably with your competitors, work out (with the buyer's help) the cost difference. It is fair to say that the customer is using your rival's price as a benchmark but also needs reassurance that your product is worth the extra investment. A couple of points worth remembering:

1. By quoting the lower price the buyer is indirectly using it as a base line. This means that you no longer have to justify the entire price of your product, you only have to justify the extra expenditure. (This is where product and competitive knowledge is essential.) List and stress all of the extra relevant benefits that the customer gets for the additional investment.
2. If the customer agrees that the additional benefits are of real value, the price disparity will no longer feature.

Do a comparison

A high-priced product does not seem quite so expensive when compared favourably with another item that is higher in price. Similarly, it is important to gather information about the performance, durability and acceptability of higher and lower priced items. In so doing, your product can be compared against the long-term benefits of your competitors.

Stress the value of the product

Make the benefits outweigh the price. The size of the price tag will be minimized or exaggerated in the eyes of the customer depending on how you emphasize the benefits.

Break down the price

Whenever buyers are trying to justify their purchase, you might be able to assist them by explaining the price the way they want to hear it. For example, you could break it into manageable amounts; instead of quoting £1,000 for an order of 10,000 units, quote the price as 10p per unit.

Another idea is to show how much the item costs in terms of time. If you are selling a desk and chair that costs £1,000, you might say that the furniture has a guaranteed life span of ten years, which works out at £16.67 per month. Supermarkets use a similar method by saying 75p per quarter rather than £3 per pound.

HOW TO PLAN THE NEGOTIATION

At the fact-finding stage, we talked about the importance of high-quality interviewing. The negotiating stage is where that information will have greatest value. For example, if you discovered that one of the unique selling points of your product or service is also an essential customer need, it adds significant weight to your negotiating stance. Good negotiation takes place before you visit the customer with your proposal and this preparation includes:

- the buyer's essential needs
- the buyer's essential needs unique to your product or service
- the concessions you are prepared to make
- the concessions you may ask of the buyer
- deciding on your top line
- deciding on the bottom line
- deciding on the location.

The buyer's essential needs

During your fact-finding the customer should have indicated (if questioned correctly) what aspects of the purchase were essential. It may have been: immediate installation or delivery; staff training on the product or service; special payment arrangements; or specific product features and benefits.

All these points should be listed in your proposal and the customer should be asked to confirm that they are consistent with his or her needs. Being able to deliver on all of these needs helps your ability to negotiate.

Buyer's essential needs unique to your product or service

If your customer confirms that your unique selling points are essential (though experienced negotiators will dilute their importance) it increases the value of your service to that particular customer.

Once again, the importance of reminding the customer of these points cannot be overstated. They should be endorsed in your proposal and listed separately to all other points.

The concessions you are prepared to make

It is essential to decide in advance of your meeting what, if any, concessions you are prepared to make if asked. Apart from your top and bottom line (see page 168) what else could you offer: better credit terms?; one year's free maintenance?; waive some charges?; free delivery or installation?; or a month's supply of consumables?

Whenever possible, give a discount in the form of a product instead of cash. A product that sells for £1000 is worth £1000 to the customer – but the cost to you may only be £500.

Concessions you may ask of the buyer

Dropping your price does not necessarily mean that you lose, you may exit with a lot more than you expected. The concessions you might ask for are: a longer contract; more volume; greater sales for your add-ons; orders from another department; better payment terms; an introduction to another buyer; or a testimonial letter.

Deciding on your own shopping list is obviously important, if the customer doesn't hassle you about price – that's a bonus.

Deciding on your top line

Once you have your package together, ensure that your documents are endorsed with the full selling price of the package. Artificially inflating the price is sharp practice and may actually cost you the business.

Deciding on the bottom line

This is a crucial figure. You decide in advance that if you can not get this price as a minimum, you are prepared to walk away without the business.

Deciding on the location

Remarkably, where you decide to meet, could be the most important part of the entire negotiation process. From my own experience, I have found that when customers are prepared to share the inconvenience of travelling to a meeting, they take it very seriously indeed. There are options open to you: invite the customer to meet you for breakfast before work!; arrange to meet at your own premises; meet at a half way location; meet in a hotel.

A few years ago, I met two businessmen in Germany who had just invested an enormous amount of money in signing the European agency for a highly successful heat pump. Three months after our initial meeting I inquired as to how business was going and this was their response.

> We took expensive advertisements in several national newspapers and visited about 30 potential distributors at their offices all over Europe. The result – not one sale! We decided to try a different approach but we couldn't afford to fly all over Europe so we asked people in France to travel to Paris and applied the same arrangement to four other locations. They didn't know we were doing this on the cheap. When we had completed our travels we had signed up 17 distributors which more than exceeded our original expectations.
>
> The only difference in the two approaches was that the second approach meant that all the distributors had to travel and those who did were genuine prospects. Furthermore, they treated our time with more respect than when we visited their offices. Now, when people want to meet us, we deliberately make it mutually inconvenient and it has worked for us.

If your customer is prepared to travel you must ensure that it is worth their while. Make sure that what you have to offer is worth the trip.

HOW TO USE NEGOTIATING SKILLS TO INCREASE SALES AND PROFITS

Anticipate the customer's questions

You can expect that a number of buyers will, in all probability, immediately ask you for your best price. You might say something such as: 'I will give you the best deal that I can! As you know these units cost £1170 each but if you are prepared to pay COD I can offer you another 5 per cent discount.'

Give and get in return

No matter what concessions you make it is vital that you get something in return, otherwise you will take all the fun out of the buying for the customer.

It's not what you concede- it's how you concede

If you offered a salesperson half of the price he had quoted for a product and he accepted, one hour later you would ask yourself: 'I wonder would he have taken a quarter of the price? Why did he give it to me so cheap? Is there something wrong with it?'

You might have got the best deal ever but your belief is that you have been conned. That makes two very unhappy people – the customer and the salesperson. Apply the same principle to your own negotiating skills, making absolutely certain that you always leave the customer with the feeling that he or she has negotiated a great deal. Give everything with polite reluctance.

Don't round off the price

Rounding the price off to an even figure (say £15,000) will be an invitation to the buyer to start negotiating. Why? Because it sounds negotiable. If the total package comes to £15,324 that should be the figure quoted.

Don't over-react to ridiculous offers

A salesperson lost an order because he embarrassed a customer by over-reacting to his offer of a 'dollar' for a product worth £6000. His inability to respond in a similar spirit may have contributed to the fact that he didn't get the sale.

Tips on face-to-face negotiation

You have to believe that everything is negotiable, and what may appear to be a constant can nearly always be converted to a variable. There is a saying: 'There hasn't been a deadline in history that wasn't negotiable':

- whenever possible, negotiate only with those in authority
- always appear to be reasonable and assure the buyer that you are prepared to offer as good a deal as you can
- remain calm throughout and look as if you are enjoying yourself. Avoid giving away your feelings by your body language and facial expression
- if you are under pressure to commit yourself to a price, take time out to phone the office. This will give you breathing space and indicate to your buyer that you are anxious to come to an arrangement
- if the buyer's offer is unacceptable you must be prepared to leave graciously without the business. The buyer may reconsider, so show there are no hard feelings and accept it as part of your job!

- tell it like it is, this is not the time to introduce indecisive language such as maybe, might be, perhaps and so on. This will put the entire negotiation at risk
- avoid getting side-tracked by discussing trivial details, try to keep focused on your negotiating objectives
- when your business is completed, leave politely and let the buyer get back to work.

TEN KEY POINTS ON NEGOTIATING PROFITABLE SALES

- Failure to sell at a profit means that all your efforts have been in vain.
- Handling customer concerns is not a competition to decide who is the smarter.
- A genuine customer concern, properly handled, is a milestone towards a sale.
- Analyse the consistency of customer comments – it aids your selling education.
- Separate objections from statements – failure to do so may cost you a sale!
- Price is only ever a deciding factor – it is rarely *the* deciding factor.
- Negotiation can be fun – provided you don't look on your buyer as an opponent.
- Plan the negotiation: decide on your top and bottom lines.
- Never give a concession without getting something in return.
- It is not *what* you concede, it is *how* you concede.

10

Building Sales on Customer Care

The primary aim of professional selling is to create customers – the primary aim of the company should be to keep them!

This chapter focuses on:

- how a lack of attention to service can create serious customer loss
- how you and your company can provide outstanding service
- how to use customer business plans to increase sales
- how to turn serious complaints into opportunities.

Customer care is the one selling activity where salespeople are at the mercy of their colleagues at head office. I have included ideas to assist you in improving the level of service that you provide to your customers.

I consider the support from within your company to be so important that I urge you to use some of the information contained in this chapter. I hope it will benefit you, your company and your customers.

First, let us look at customer service, why it can go wrong, and some suggestions as to how it can be put right!

HOW A LACK OF ATTENTION TO SERVICE CAN CREATE SERIOUS CUSTOMER LOSS

In relation to your levels of customer service:

- Do you know (or anybody else in your organization) exactly how many customers you lost in the past twelve months?
- Do you know why you have lost them?
- Do you have an established complaints procedure?
- Is the procedure effective?
- Does everyone in your company see themselves as part of a sales team?
- Does your company have regular staff training in customer service?
- If you answer 'no' to any of these questions, you may well be passing business on to your competitors.

'We give outstanding service'

If there is one thing that unites practically all salespeople, it is that they give outstanding service. If there is one thing that unites practically all customers it is that they cannot get outstanding service. When was the last time you received outstanding service consistently from any company? (Most people are hard pressed to identify one.)

Service is perception

There is often an enormous disparity between the service we provide and the customer's perceptions of the service received. One way to address this issue is to carry out your own research. There are four areas of service in which a salesperson requires accurate information:

1. The level of service expected by the customer.
2. The current level of service given by the salesperson.

3. The service levels provided by the 'company sales team'.
4. The level of service provided by your competitors.

This research does not require a six-month sabbatical, the key information will come from being vigilant in competitive activity and asking all your customers: 'What level of service do you expect from me and my company?' or 'What are we not doing for you that we could or should be doing?'

How customers are lost

The importance of uncovering customer expectations of service is underlined by Dun and Bradstreets' investigations into customer loss. Their enquiries revealed that 16 out of every 100 customers stop buying every year for the following reasons:

- 1 per cent die
- 3 per cent change jobs or move away
- 5 per cent favour friends
- 9 per cent change for better prices
- 82 per cent are unhappy with suppliers.

There may be little we can do to save the first 18 per cent, but the other 82 per cent are very much within the clawback capability of most organizations. By doing so you not only help to swell company profits but you are also securing your own job.

How retailers lose 57 per cent

An even more disturbing survey was carried out on customer loss in the retail trade. It claimed that for every 100 customers, 57 are lost in the first three years of setting up a business for the following reasons: moved away; indifferent treatment; poor quality; poor service; and grievances are not settled to customers' satisfaction.

If everyone is claiming that they provide excellent service, how come it is still the biggest cause of customer loss? In competitive markets customers have a choice. If we can not give them what they are looking for, they can always find it somewhere else.

The selling effort required to replace lost customers

Let us assume that you have a customer base of 300 and you are losing them at the rate of 16 per cent per year. Let us also assume that you have been given a target to increase the number of customers by 10 per cent. Consider this: to increase your customer base from 300 to 330 is not a 10 per cent increase; because you are still losing 48 customers (16 per cent), you now need to win another 78 customers. In real terms this is an increase of 23.4 per cent.

Of the 16 per cent that you will lose, remember that the majority of those losses can be avoided by better customer service from you and your colleagues.

THE HIDDEN COSTS OF POOR SERVICE

It must be easier to hold on to an old customer than to find a new one. Research indicates it is also up to five times less expensive. It is difficult to calculate the actual cost of customer loss through bad service but it probably involves: costs of legal action or advice; loss of a sale or customer; loss of sales due to bad publicity; cost of replacing the business that has been lost.

Add to this the frustration for the salesperson and the need to find another customer – just to stand still!

THE SALES TEAM

Have a look at the map of Europe (see Figure 10.1) and without reading any further, see if you can work out the message the illustration is intended to convey.

Figure 10.1 *The Sales Team*

I used this illustration to make a point to a company looking for a fire brigade solution to serious customer service problems, in spite of the fact that they only sold within their own national boundaries. Much to their amusement, I placed the various departments all over Europe, and told them how I saw their organization. Each of the divisions within their company spoke a different customer language and each department had its own objectives to achieve – most of which did not involve the relationship with the customer as a consideration.

The inter-departmental exchange of customer information was so poor that the departments may as well have been operating in different countries. This company had several departments communicating with the customer yet no system of communicating with each other. The reason: 'We have enough to do without having to duplicate our conversations.'

The main problem here is that managers were getting caught in the crossfire between achieving sales, making a profit and looking after customers. A company unable to sort out where its priorities lie will do little for harmonious relations with the customer.

Could this happen in your company?

I believe that the above example applies to many companies. Companies cannot afford to be selective to whom they give customer service training. It may be expensive, but it will never be as expensive as losing customers.

Salespeople are customer-driven and their communication will tend to be polite and courteous. Company personnel, unaware of their 'selling' role and not tutored in diplomacy may offend customers with things such as: 'No point in you shouting at me – I only work here'; 'You will have to phone back again – he's too busy to take your call'; or 'Put your complaint in writing and we will deal with it as soon as we can.'

Sales and service tend to have different objectives. When I talk to salespeople about after-sales service they often say: 'If those people in head office only realized how difficult it is to get the order in the first place, they might be a little more supportive.' When I talk to the service department they respond with: 'It's OK for him to talk about support, if he quoted realistic delivery dates we wouldn't be under so much pressure.' This kind of internal bickering results in customer aggravation and eventual loss of business.

Everyone in the organization has a selling role

It is a simple fact of business – everyone in the company sells, from the chief executive to the part-time school-leaver in the canteen. Selling, no matter how effective, will have no long-term benefits for your company if there is not a high 'customer care' awareness – enthusiastically demonstrated by salespeople and supported throughout the organization.

'If only customers stopped ringing I could get my work done'

An understandable difficulty with many indoor staff (and managers for that matter) is that they rarely consider anything other than the role they were employed to do. For example, if you ask a staff member to tell you what their job is, don't be surprised to hear: 'To answer the phone and take messages'; 'To pack the shelves'; 'To keep the department running smoothly'; or 'To deliver the goods'.

Each response highlights a total absence of a customer dimension and the reason? They were never told otherwise. If staff are properly trained they would respond with: 'My job is to... with a view to providing the best service for the customers.'

How the finance department can cause customer loss

It never ceases to amaze me that so many financial people fail to recognize the input their department can have on sales. Although it is rarely a financial person's function to get customers, their behaviour can certainly lose them. Take this lose/lose letter from a financial institution to one of its clients:

> Your account is in arrears. Unless we hear from you within the next seven days we will be forced to take legal action.

> This action will incur legal costs of £300 for which you will be personally liable.
>
> PS (the final insult): If you have paid your account within the past few days, please ignore this notice.

If this was the last in a series of reminders, the language used might be understandable. In this particular case, it was the second appeal letter the customer received.

The bad news circle

Bad news travels fast, and the business world is not a metropolis where people don't know each other – it's a village where people talk to each other. If you were planning a wedding and you invited all the people that you know, it is claimed that the average list will extend to 200 names. A buyer badly treated by a supplier might eventually get that message to those 200 people. To put it in a nutshell: 'When I do something wrong, everybody knows about it, when I do something right nobody is around to see me doing it.'

Our 24-hour marketing role

Business is not only lost between nine and five: it can be lost in the evenings or at weekends. For example, people with access to company transport should at all times display good driving manners and keep the vehicle clean and tidy. Also, when people talk socially about their jobs, all too often their comments are anything but complimentary about their service, company or colleagues.

A customer told me he had decided to install aluminium windows in his house, and had selected a company to do the job. Late one Saturday evening he was driving out of the city when another driver flashed his lights, blew his horn and made aggressive gestures. Blinded by the headlights, my acquaintance pulled over to let the van pass, as he did so, the driver mouthed obscenities at him. However, the car owner noticed the name on the van: it was the aluminium company with whom he had been in the process of doing business. In spite of all the gracious apologies offered by the salesperson, his company lost the business.

Companies invest heavily in sales teams to win business, but sloppy, uncaring staff oblivious to their 24-hour marketing role will squander any gains. The irony is that the employees involved are being paid good money while losing business. It is vital for management to impress upon all employees the importance of maintaining the company's image at all times. Every company should have proper forums where staff can communicate with each other and relate ideas back to management on how jobs, conditions and customer service can be improved!

HOW YOU AND YOUR COMPANY CAN PROVIDE OUTSTANDING SERVICE

How well do you know your customers?

How much do you know about your average customer? Select any customer at random and answer as many of the following questions as you can. On completion of the exercise, calculate the points you have scored (grades given below).

Do you know?	*Yes*	*No*
The customer's full name (spelling and pronunciation)		
Full title (managing director, sales manager, etc)		
His background		
Length of time with his present company		
His interests and hobbies		
The receptionist's name		

Do you know?	*Yes*	*No*
Porter/security guard's name		
General manager/chief executive's name		
Customer's assistant's name		
The customer's company's full range of products		
The customer's competitors in the market		
The company's origin		
Whether they have branch offices or associate companies		
Number of employees in the company		
Which of your rival companies he also deals with		
The best time of the day to call		
His motives for buying your product		
What unique selling points would be of benefit to him		
What experience he has had with your rivals		

Scores
Score 10 points for every 'yes' answer. You score as follows:

150-200 – excellent
120-150 – good, but could be improved
90-120 – average. Probably reflected in the sales results.
50-90 – below average. Weak relationship with this customer.
0-50 – very poor. Do you really care about this customer?

How you can bring about a change in service

It is difficult for you as a salesperson to change in-bred company attitudes overnight. But you maybe able to do some of the following:

- Ask senior management to allow you to make a presentation to them on the need for improved customer service. Use whatever ideas you require from this book to support your message.

- Set up customer panels and invite a cross-section of your market to offer opinions or guidance on how service levels could be improved.
- Encourage your company to set up a task force to address the important issues of customer care.
- Follow the suggestions on proactive service (see pp 202m/s)

Fifteen seconds to prove you are the best

Apply the positive experiences of another customer-driven company, SAS. Jan Carlzon, president of Scandinavian Airlines, in his book *Moments of Truth,* claimed that in one year his staff came in contact with 10 million customers approximately five times. The contact lasted on average 15 seconds each time. He goes on to say: 'Thus, SAS is created in the minds of our customers 50 million times a year, 15 seconds at a time. They are the moments when we must prove to our customers that SAS is the best alternative.'

As salespeople, we should recognize the importance of responding to a changing market-place. Attitudes are continuously changing and customer-driven companies such as SAS are showing the way forward.

How a change of job title can help improve service

Earlier we discussed the dangers of staff not extending their thinking to include a customer dimension, but would they do so automatically, if they had change of job title? For example, converting a 'Sales Assistant' to a 'Customer Assistant' will obviously not change the overall job specification but it might change the job holder's perception of where the emphasis should be placed, and the customers.

The spirit of 'yes I can' to positive service

Recently, on a trip to the United States, I stayed at the Radisson Hotel, and as I entered the hotel I noticed that all the staff (including the manager) were wearing badges with 'Yes, I can' written on them. All communications with patrons started with 'Yes I can, so how can I help you?' This may be gimmicky, but I was impressed by the efficiency and friendliness of the staff.

If we could all greet customers with the same positive mental attitude (not necessarily verbalized) the impact on the growth of the business would be dynamic.

The need for proactive service

Proactive customer care is an attitude that must come from a realization that this is the way to build a relationship. Unhappily, in our profession, everything we promise in advance of the sale is subject to cynicism and suspicion, and only a series of positive experiences will convince customers that there are no strings attached to the service.

Looking after your customers' customers

There are a number of activities that a salesperson can carry out as part of an everyday proactive customer care campaign. Here are a few suggestions.

The buyer and the user of your product or services may be two different people, so establish and maintain contact with both parties, they are of equal importance to you.

Make contact with a user and a buyer every day. If appropriate, follow up with a brief note. For example: 'Thank you for taking the time to talk to me this morning. I am pleased that your new laser printer is working so efficiently. Since yours was installed, we have introduced a new user manual which I think may be of interest to you.'

I like to think that I practice what I preach. As part of my service I try to contact as many delegates as possible after a course. I learn much from these conversations. It is worthwhile reminding you that these people are users and not buyers.

One of the most mutually beneficial relationships that I have formed has resulted from the buyer's reaction to my post-course service. He offered me a long-term training contract, and his reason was this: 'The fact that you provided this valuable service without charge or expectation speaks volumes for you and your company.' (He concluded his remarks with a telling comment for all of us in selling: 'We are not used to this level of service.' I should make the point that this man is a buyer in one of the world's largest telecommunications companies.)

When a customer buys!

I believe that most salespeople would automatically thank customers for the business at the time of being given the order. Few, in my experience, write a special note to say thank you, such as: 'This is a brief note to thank you for the business that you passed on to me. I do appreciate it!'

What is important about this letter is that the only motivation for writing was to express gratitude for the order, and the spirit is not diluted by including invoices, brochures or selling details.

When a customer doesn't buy!

We can never look on losing an order as the end of the relationship; on the contrary it may well signal the start of a new one. A brief note could work wonders in future dealings:

> 'I was sorry to learn that we are not going to do business on this occasion. Nevertheless, I am grateful to you for your time and interest!'
>
> Continued success.

Little things can make a big difference!

Customers appreciate thoughtful gestures and friendship. There is no reason why we should not be prepared to assist the customer outside of our own product or service. Think in terms of their problems, for example, is there any information you can also provide that would help him or her?

If you come across information that you know will be of interest to a customer, send it with a compliment slip. I sent a customer a cutting from a magazine, which related to a project he was working on. He telephoned to thank me – the information was invaluable!

You may also find that you can keep customers posted on competitive conditions in their industry or provide updates on purchases. Instead of sending the usual Christmas gift of alcohol or calendars, try to find something of particular interest to that buyer. Remember it is not the cost of the gift that is really important to most people – it is the thought that goes into its choice.

A service role for senior people

Senior management have a major customer care role, though typically they only become involved with customers when the business is all but lost, or there is some other problem. It's surprising but true that most senior executives never communicate directly with customers.

Bring on the heavyweights!

The most powerful and influential people in any company are the senior executives and the power of their presence and support in the selling effort can never be overstated. How would it be perceived by the customer if the chief executive was to:

- Phone customers personally to thank them for their business?
- Write a personal letter expressing gratitude?
- After the product or service has been delivered, call in to ensure everything is alright?
- Do a PR visit to one customer per week for the purpose of listening to what they have to say?

If four senior managers made one telephone call per day to a customer to thank them for the business, at the end of the year 1000 customers might actually believe that you care!

Financial controller

Earlier we discussed the negative impact on customers who receive badly-worded lose/lose reminders from the anonymous person in the finance department. Supposing •this same person wrote to a customer thus: 'You have been dealing with us for many years and I trust that we provide you with an efficient back-up service! As the financial controller, I cannot help but notice that you always attend to our invoices promptly. I want you to know that we appreciate your courtesy and your business. If you ever have any queries I do hope you will contact me personally.'

While accounts departments spend a lot of money trying to collect bad debts, few in my experience, will invest in a telephone call or a letter to thank those who do pay on time!

Care is more than just a few words

Recently I stood in the reception area of a major organization, reading an eloquently-worded mission statement, telling me how much they cared about me as a customer. I would like to have asked the author of the document: If the company was indeed sincere about what they had written, how was it that all the parking spaces outside the building were allotted to senior management and staff, forcing customers to trade excuses with the traffic warden?

In all customer-driven companies, it is essential that all staff and management embrace a customer care philosophy. It is pointless for any person to draw up a set of operating procedures without the commitment to these ideas by all staff.

MISSION STATEMENTS

A mission statement is a document that should be signed by all staff. In a retail store it might read as follows:

Mission Statement

It is our promise to:
provide convenience shopping to satisfy your needs;
offer fast friendly and efficient service;
upkeep our store to the highest possible level of hygiene;
provide a consistently high level of quality goods.

If however, you feel our service could be improved, please notify any of our customer service team.

If you put a notice like this on display, ensure that every employee adheres to the principles or it will lessen your credibility.

The benefits of teamwork

In the final analysis, the test of an organization is the performance given by the company team. Like all teams, it is only successful when everyone strives to achieve a common goal. Our role is to lift our vision to higher levels, to raise performance to higher standards and help build team effort beyond its normal limitations: executives set the standards; managers show by example; staff imitate their performance; and customers evaluate the harmony of all the relationships.

A company that ignores these basic ideas breeds contempt for its own survival and destroys its greatest resource – its people.

HOW TO USE CUSTOMER BUSINESS PLANS TO INCREASE SALES

As I work closely with salespeople and their customers, I see at first hand the difficulties both the salesperson and the customer have in sustaining a positive relationship. In my view, there is a serious anomaly between what the customer would like the salesperson to do and what the salesperson actually does. Salespeople are often seen more as predators than partners in increasing sales and profitability. Because of these 'perceptions' both people communicate as if they were opponents.

We all have a number of buyers who fit into the 'difficult customer category' and if this scenario also applies to you I would strongly urge you to consider a radical change of approach.

Building better relationships with established customers

I don't know what industry you work in, but if it is possible to apply the following skills to your annual sales campaign then I urge you to do so! If, on the other hand, you have a few difficult customers where your relationship with them is hindering your ability to sell, these very same principles (with some minor alteration) will help considerably. Here are a few useful hints:

- Write out a list of all those customers where a change in the relationship or customer attitude would benefit both parties.
- Instead of your usual sales visit, telephone the customer and explain that you have some important new ideas that will help to increase sales that you would like to discuss (give as little detail as possible).

It is essential that you arrange to meet away from the customer's premises, for breakfast, coffee or lunch. This helps to reinforce the message that this conversation is different.

Pre-planning is critical

It this stage your customer will be intrigued as to the sudden change in approach, therefore your meeting must meet his or her expectations. Write down exactly what you wish to say as an opener and make sure that it is worded in the interest of the customer. Pre-planning their questions is a critical part of the exercise. Perhaps you can use some of the following:

- What can I or my company do to help you to improve your sales or profitability?
- What level of sales would you like to achieve?
- What would you like me to do on my visits?
- How often do you want me to call?
- What is the best time to call on you?

Remember that the purpose of this meeting is only to get information and even if the customer makes an outrageous request avoid discussing it at this stage.

Designing the win/win business plan

Designing and presenting the business plan is a matter of personal choice. Depending on the complexity of your product or service it may range from one sheet of paper to a 12-page document. I propose that you keep it as simple as possible. In one retail business that I am associated with it fits on two pages and outlines the following:

These retailers are delighted that other people are taking such a positive interest in the overall development of their business. Relationships have improved dramatically and both customer and salesperson are trying to achieve the same common goal.

Business Plan

Sales achievement	**Year ending 31/12/98**	**Increase of X per cent over last year**
Projected sales	**Year ending 31/12/99**	**Actual sales to date**

Store development goals 1999/2000

Store objectives	**Goal to be achieved**	**Finish date**	**Who will do it?**
Marketing			
Customer service			
Corporate image			
Sales targets			
Per square foot			
Per staff member			
Per department			
Merchandising			
Special promotions			
Staff training			
Hygiene			

Sales visit: first Monday of every month at 8.30 am

Call objectives

Objectives for next call

According to the salespeople who have tried this approach the most amazing transformation was the enormous change in customer attitude. They no longer looked at the salespeople as opponents, but partners in profitability, and their time was treated with much more respect. Try it, it really does work!

HOW TO TURN SERIOUS COMPLAINTS INTO OPPORTUNITIES

There are few greater satisfactions for a salesperson than to receive a serious complaint and turn the situation into one where the customer emerges with greater confidence and trust in the salesperson and the company. Customers have a choice: they can bring their complaints directly to you or they can go straight to your competitors. Some important points to bear in mind:

- No matter how serious a complaint is, it is what happens next that is of most importance to the customer.
- Look on complaints as 'situations' and not insurmountable problems – this will help you to keep focused on a solution.
- When a customer complains, regardless of how they explain themselves, remember their motivation is to have the complaint resolved – the anger should be seen as secondary.
- Most heated complaints have their roots in the fear that 'all is lost'. If you can calmly reassure the customer that you will put it right – they will become more conciliatory in their attitude.

Recording complaints

Anybody can record a complaint, but it takes a caring professional to turn it around. If the situation is resolved to the customer's satisfaction, you may be on the way to a better relationship than ever before. It is nice to hear people say: 'OK, so I had a problem but in fairness they resolved it better and quicker than I expected.'

Nip the complaint in the bud!

While I have listed 20 ways to handle complaints, carrying out this simple exercise will prevent a drama from developing into a crisis. When you are informed of a complaint it is essential that you telephone the customer immediately and acknowledge that you have received it. This is a key issue. What it will achieve is:

- The customer knows that you have just received the complaint, and will hardly expect an instant solution.

- Your efficient response will eliminate a major cause of customer aggravation 'what the hell are they doing about my complaint?'
- You can test the temperature and take corrective action.
- You can express your regret for the cause of the complaint and reassure the customer that you will resolve the difficulty within a certain time.

The biggest mistake that people make when handling serious complaints is to fuel the fire of annoyance by not getting back to the customer quickly enough. Applying this principle will not eliminate serious complaints, but it will make them easier to handle.

TWENTY BETTER WAYS TO HANDLE COMPLAINTS AND ARGUMENTS

'You have not converted a man because you have silenced him.' (John Morley) Everyone knows that you cannot win arguments, yet so many people try. Company personnel come into contact with many different people every day. Those people will have their day brightened or darkened by the manner, attitude and tone of the employees' greeting and communication skills.

The ability to communicate another point of view to someone who is highly emotional is a very important skill, which can be learnt. The following are 20 skills that work; regardless of how emotional, hysterical or placid the other person may be, the same rules apply.

1. Don't argue. Arguments leave both parties beaten and drained and the subsequent atmosphere is rarely conducive to selling or good communication.
2. Don't try to 'win'. Even if you win, you will lose – if not the respect and support of colleagues and friends, then quite likely the sale, and possibly one of your best customers.

3. Don't compete with customers' opinions. An argument is a challenge to another person's 'emotional judgement' and you will rarely change someone's opinion once you have challenged that judgement.
4. Expect customers to be annoyed. Do not expect the customer to be in a rational frame of mind. Anger frequently accompanies a complaint.
5. Avoid being casual. Maintain a professional approach. The customer is likely to be oversensitive to a casual or uncaring attitude.
6. See complaints as opportunities. Complaints are an opportunity to demonstrate the high standards of professionalism employed by your company.
7. Take responsibility. Do not pass the buck. Take personal responsibility to ensure the complaint or query is completed to the customer's satisfaction.
8. Care. Show you really do care by your actions, manner and personal interest in resolving the query.
9. Listen, listen, listen. A most important skill in handling conflict is the ability to listen with all your senses. Avoid trying to calm the other person down, this will only make the situation worse.
10. Remain calm. Try to maintain your cool. Ensure your body language or telephone reaction is not conveying anger or shock. This will encourage the other person to get it 'off their chest'. Do not allow yourself to be drawn into an argument.
11. Never interrupt. Apart from being the height of bad manners, it will only add to the other person's annoyance. Respond when appropriate and use expressions such as: 'I see', 'I understand', or 'I agree'.
13. Ask appropriate questions. The only way you can demonstrate your 'real interest' in others' points of view is by asking questions. Take notes as you go along for the purpose of summarizing when appropriate. Ask open-ended questions such as why, what, when, etc.
14. Ignore remarks or insults. When people are angry they occasionally say things they don't really mean.

Customers may say things such as: 'I have already told you that, are you deaf?'; or 'How stupid you people are!' It is foolish to take these comments personally and nothing is to be gained from drawing a new issue into the discussion. When the situation is resolved the customer will usually apologize for his remarks. Ignore the insults and ask some appropriate question about the main issue. Developing this skill requires patience and tremendous self-discipline, but it is worth it.

15. Wait for calmness. Experience indicates that people can not shout at the top of their voices forever – they will eventually calm down. Usually, your courtesy in listening will be reciprocated. If the other person does interrupt you, it probably means that you have not given him enough time to explain himself. In any event, try to avoid embarrassing the other person with the 'political cliche' – 'I didn't interrupt you, so please don't interrupt me.'
16. Summarize the points at issue. Demonstrate your understanding of the issues by summarizing: 'If I understand you correctly, this is the situation… ' Make sure the customer agrees with your interpretation.

Empathy allows us to understand without having to agree. Bearing in mind that the complaint may be based on a lack of information on the customer's part, saying he or she is wrong or that you don't agree, is not likely to help an already difficult situation. Empathy is expressed thus: 'I can understand how you feel about it, Mr Customer, and if I were in that situation I am sure I would be just as annoyed; however, there is another viewpoint which I would ask you to consider… '

Avoid a situation where a salesperson has to say 'I disagree with you' or 'We will have to agree to differ.' By mentioning 'disagreement' you are highlighting the fact that you are in conflict.

17. Find an area of agreement and state it. Rarely will a customer have it so wrong that there are no areas for agree-

ment. Even conceding a small point may add to a conciliatory atmosphere: 'Mr Customer, I agree with you: if we said we would deliver on Tuesday and you did not receive it until Thursday, that is totally unacceptable and I would be just as angry.' Alternatively, if you or your company are at fault for the entire complaint, apologize, get it out of the way and take the appropriate action. Customers accept that things do go wrong now and then; the critical point is how the complaint is handled.

18. Demonstrate empathy. Customers do not always expect you to agree with them but what all of them can justifiably expect is that you will do your utmost to understand their point of view.
19. Agree on action or follow-up. Whatever agreement is made between you and the customer should be followed up with all speed. Complaints are an inevitable part of business but how they are handled will dictate your company's future relationship with the customer.
20. Thank the customer for the complaint. The customer has a choice: to bring the complaint directly to you, or take it to your competitor. Those who bring their complaints directly to you should be thanked. Sometimes a brief note to the customer, thanking him or her for taking the time to contact you and giving you the opportunity to correct it will do a lot for the business relationship. Many people protest by taking their business elsewhere.

What is a customer?

- A customer is the most important person ever to contact us, in person, by mail or telephone.
- A customer is not dependent on us. We are dependent on the customer.
- A customer is not an interruption of your work – he or she is the purpose of it.
- We are not doing the customer a favour by serving him – the customer is doing us a favour by allowing us to do so!

- Customers are not cold statistics, they are human beings with feelings and emotions like our own.
- A customer is not someone with whom to match wits. Nobody ever won an argument with a customer.
- Customers are people who bring us their wants and needs. It is our job to cater for them, thereby profiting the customer, the company and ourselves!

TEN KEY POINTS TO BUILDING SALES ON CUSTOMER CARE

- Most of the business that we lose could be avoided.
- Everybody in the company sells – get them on your side!
- Enlist the support of senior management to improve customer care.
- Service is more than just a few words – it has to be followed by action.
- Give a little extra – go above and beyond the sale!
- Changing a job title may help staff change their perceptions.
- Look after your customers' customers.
- A complaint is never as important as to what happens next.
- Complaints are an opportunity to increase customer goodwill.
- By making customers' problems your problems, you become more than a salesperson – you become a friend!

11

Increasing Selling Productivity

There is a world of difference between working hard and working smart. This module sets out to help you to maximize the use of your most precious resource – time. This chapter covers how to:

- find out where your time goes
- know how to eliminate time-wasting activities
- maximize the use of selling time.

FINDING OUT WHERE YOUR TIME GOES

Time robbers

Have a look at the following list of time robbers and put a tick against all the tasks that frequently eat into your time. Be absolutely honest with yourself if there are other activities that could be influencing your selling time, note them.

Notorious time robbers in selling

- bad territory management, ie back-tracking, hopping from one side of the city to the other

- lack of planning
- no systematic approach to calls
- making fixed appointments where more flexible times might have been acceptable
- writing when a telephone call will do
- calling in person when a letter or telephone call will suffice
- spending too much time on the telephone
- extended lunch and coffee breaks
- socializing with colleagues during business hours
- finishing work early
- starting late
- giving sales presentations to the wrong people.

You may well include many company-imposed time-wasters, but do not allow yourself to get caught up in the crossfire between what you are paid to do, ie spend time at meetings, and what you are not paid to do – waste time socializing with colleagues.

If you could convert the percentage of time loss into a corresponding increase in sales, how much more money would you have earned last year? What would you have been able to do with the extra money? Take a holiday? Reduce your mortgage payments? Extra cash in the bank earning interest?

Time activity analysis

Find out where your time is spent and work with determination to eliminate time-wasting activities. Refer to Figure 11.1 and carry out the following analysis over the next ten days. If the result is inconclusive, repeat it for a further ten days. Each block represents 15 minutes and each line, seven working hours.

Activity	Time spent on activities																				Total
Time in office																					
Paper work/admin																					
Meetings/training																					
Talking to colleagues																					
Coffee breaks																					
Telephone queries																					
Telephone appointments																					
Telephone sales																					
Telephone · personal																					
Driving · travelling																					
Backtracking																					
Waiting on buyers																					
Selling to wrong people																					
Face-to-face selling																					
Small talk to buyers																					
Post call activity																					
Personal business																					
Phoning back to office																					
Other activities																					
Leadership skills																					
Miscellaneous																					

Figure 11.1 *Time activity analysis*

HOW TO ELIMINATE TIME WASTING ACTIVITIES

Good territory management means: seeing as many of the right people – at the right time, under the best conditions, at the least possible cost, and getting maximum sales, from every suitable outlet.

Professional salespeople can improve sales by perfecting selling methods. Another excellent way to increase sales is to scrutinize and guard time. Only when you know what your time is worth and how to evaluate the cost of what you do is it possible to reach conclusions as to how to increase face-to-face selling time.

If you saw a colleague throw £500 straight into the fire, you would consider it a dreadful waste. Yet, most of us will waste at least 25 per cent of our selling time doing non-productive things. You can waste time or kill time, or you can save it prudently and invest it wisely.

Ten valuable time saving tips

As you progress through these questions score ten points for every one that you are currently doing and see how you rate on completion.

1. The first step to managing time is to identify your daily goals and priorities. Have a definite plan of action to achieve them. Organize your day in a manner which achieves maximum effectiveness.
2. Plan your work and work your plan. Some people believe that planning is merely deciding what to do in the future. However, a better definition of planning, particularly in selling, is deciding what you have to do in order to have a future.
3. Distinguish between efficiency and effectiveness. All too often we confuse the two. Efficiency is doing the job right whereas effectiveness is doing the right job. Effectiveness means results.

NAME	DEPT.	DATE
MUST DO	SHOULD DO	TELEPHONE
		CALL TO
APPOINTMENTS	MEETINGS	
		PERSONAL

Figure 11.2 *Day Planner*

4. Remember Parkinson's Law: 'Work expands to fill the time available.' Reduce the time available and the job will still get done.
5. Analyse the quality of your calls. Spend your time on activities or potential customers who are likely to yield the best results or are worth the task. Look for obvious time-wasters and eliminate them.
6. Write out a daily action list and keep to it. Do not tackle low priority tasks until all the high priority tasks have been completed.(see Day Planner on page 202)
7. Listen to self-development material in the car when travelling. Save time by training outside business hours. Keep trade magazines in your briefcase to read while waiting at reception for buyers.
8. Carry a thermos flask and sandwiches when travelling, particularly to remote parts of your territory.
9. Where possible, handle small, marginal accounts by telephone. (see 80/20 rule on page 206)
10. Many salespeople sell only between the hours of nine and five, Monday to Friday. A reasonable number of customers are available before nine and after five. Every call made during these times increases the potential for better results. Some customers may be delighted with an invitation to breakfast, lunch, or an evening meal.

You score as follows:

80 plus: if that is a genuine score, your time management is excellent
60 plus: work with determination to build on your ratings
40 plus: this is how the majority of salespeople score before taking action
20 plus: a lot of work to do!

MAXIMIZE SELLING TIME

No matter how you look at it, there are only two ways to increase your sales: sell more customers, or sell customers more.

The key is selling productivity, and time and sound territory management is a critical element. Your 'territory' may not be geographical; it may be a series of designated accounts, a specific market segment or an area defined by telephone prefix/area codes.

The epitome of designing an excellent selling campaign is how you manage all of your resources to maximize productivity and ensure outstanding customer service. The amateur salesperson looks at the selling 'patch' as a list of prospects, whereas professionals take a wider view and look on it as they would a small business – taking personal responsibility for everything that happens on that 'territory'.

So little time to sell!

Many companies, realizing the importance of cost effectiveness, have conducted surveys on their salespeople's territory management. They claim that it works out as follows:

- travel – 35 per cent
- waiting – 15 per cent
- administration – 16 per cent
- sales meetings – 10 per cent
- face-to-face selling – 24 per cent.

To some salespeople this 24 per cent face-to-face figure appears outrageous but when they complete their time analysis they are shocked at how much they have overestimated their selling time. If you have never reviewed your time management, I believe that you will also be amazed by the end of this chapter!

If it were possible for you to increase your selling time from 24 per cent to 32 per cent, you would in effect be increasing selling potential by 33 per cent.

In money terms this means that if you presently earn £30,000, through better time management you could increase those earnings to £40,000 – without working any harder.

The cost per sales call

Whatever salary and commission you earn, that figure can be doubled when you add all the accompanying overheads. One such case that comes to mind is where I assisted a sales team to improve their time management. We agreed that with holidays, sickness, training and time in the office they actually spent about 100 days per year out on their territory.

They were scheduled to do five calls per day but in reality it worked out at no more than three. This worked out at 300 calls per year and an approximate cost of £330 per call. It suddenly becomes very important to make every call count.

How much are you worth?

From Table 11.1 work out the true cost of losing one hour per day. Based on a 233 working days per year at seven working hours per day, your time can be calculated as follows:

Table 11.2 *Cost of losing one hour per day*

Total cost to the company pa £	*Each hour is worth* £	*The loss of one hour per day per year* £
5,000	*3.06*	*714*
6,000	*3.67*	*857*
7,000	*4.29*	*1,000*
8,000	*4.90*	*1,142*
9,000	*5.51*	*1,285*
10,000	*6.13*	*1,428*
11,000	*6.74*	*1,571*
12,000	*7.35*	*1,714*

13,000	*7.97*	*1,857*
14,000	*8.58*	*2,000*
15,000	*9.19*	*2,142*
16,000	*9.80*	*2,285*
17,000	*10.42*	*2,428*
18,000	*11.03*	*2,571*
19,000	*11.64*	*2,714*
20,000	*12.26*	*2,875*
25,000	*15.32*	*3,571*
30,000	*18.39*	*4,285*
35,000	*21.45*	*4,999*
40,000	*24.52*	*5,713*

The 80/20 rule

A very important guide as to how you spend your time is the Pareto Principle, called after the 19th century Italian economist. It is often referred to as the 80/20 rule. In selling terms it means:

- 80 per cent of your sales will come from 20 per cent of your customers
- 20 per cent of your sales will come from 80 per cent of your customers.

In your case it could be 70/30, 60/40 or even 90/10 but whatever the figure, it is essential to identify who your top customers are because they are the people who give you most of your annual sales target.

Generally, the 80/20 rule will apply to everything you do in selling. You will find that 80 per cent of your complaints will come from 20 per cent of your customers and 80 per cent of your efforts will result in 20 per cent of your sales. In essence, we should concentrate on those activities likely to yield the best results!

The Pareto Principle

The 80/20 rule has some interesting aspects for salespeople and selling in general. In many cases it can be much worse than 80/20. At 90/10, this puts the entire selling operation at the mercy of a small number of customers. Consider the following example.

I worked as a consultant with a small company with six salespeople who were talking to a lot of customers and not getting a lot of sales. Applying the Pareto Principle to their sales analysis I discovered they had 520 key customers (or so they thought) and every customer got a call once a month.

Customer service did not discriminate – every customer got the same lousy service.

I was hired because they were losing customers and money, complaints were being badly handled, salespeople were under a lot of stress and something had to be done. The subsequent analysis was frightening for all concerned.

- three of their 520 customers gave them 45 per cent of their annual turnover
- 46 customers gave them 25 per cent
- the remaining 471 gave them 20 per cent.

Anyone looking at these figures can see immediately that this company was in a very vulnerable situation. If those top three customers were to take their business elsewhere, this company would have folded under the strain of its running costs. The solution was simple – I put all the customers into different categories.

Grade A customers: these were only three, but vitally important, accounts. One salesperson was given special responsibility for all contact, including customer service. This individual now had plenty of time to canvass new major accounts – something he could not do in the past.

Grade B customers: with better territory planning this only required one salesperson and the customers were getting a far better service.

Of the remaining 471 (giving 20 per cent of the business) we were able to grade them as follows:

Grade C customers: 67 customers representing 10 per cent of the annual turnover, but with potential for development.
Grade D customers: 120 requiring a call every three months. All C and D customers to be handled by one person.
Grade E Customers: it was agreed that it was costing money to have a salesperson calling on these customers and they should be handled by telephone.

It was accepted that some personal visits would be inevitable. Because of the way it was explained to these customers no-one had a problem with the change of selling policy.

The downside of this arrangement meant that two salespeople were made redundant, but as it happened, one moved to replace a manager who was leaving and the other moved to another company. As salespeople were taking responsibility for service, two of the three customer service team were also made redundant.

The benefits to this company were considerable. They immediately saved over £180,000 in direct selling costs by reducing the sales team by 30 per cent (this included cars, phones and the costs of servicing 284 monthly sales calls). The customer service team was reduced by 66 per cent, and the sales team were more focused on what they were trying to achieve. Customers were getting a better service, and the company needed £1,200,000 less in sales because of the reductions in staffing levels and service calls.

We should all learn from this experience and constantly appraise who gives us the business. Make absolutely certain that you use your skills to give your customers outstanding service while at the same time giving you enough time to develop your sales.

Exercise

Look at the exercises you have completed in this section on Increasing Selling Productivity. What are the main learning points for you? What action do you need to take?

TEN KEY POINTS ON INCREASING SELLING PRODUCTIVITY

- Effectiveness versus efficiency – doing the right job and doing the job right.
- Only two ways to increase sales – sell more customers or sell customers more.
- There is a world of difference between working hard and working smart.
- Plan your work and work your plan – inspect what you expect.
- Most salespeople could dramatically increase earnings – without extra efforts.
- If you earn £40,000 – losing one hour a day has cost you £5,713.
- Remember the 80/20 rule – work on tasks yielding most profitable results.
- Do not tackle low priority tasks until high priority tasks have been completed.
- Good territory management – seeing the right people at the right time.
- Work out the cost of your average sales call – it will motivate a new attitude.

12

Generating New Business

One thing is sure – if you don't have a constant supply of live leads and if you fail to see prospects, you won't have any new business. In this chapter we look at:

- how to increase your prospects of getting new customers
- how to maximize your prospects of meeting buyers
- how to maximize sales through proper use of the telephone.

HOW TO INCREASE YOUR PROSPECTS OF GETTING NEW CUSTOMERS

Prospecting is an integral part of the salesperson's plan and must be carried out regularly to ensure a constant source of new contacts. You will find leads in a variety of areas, but bear in mind that most other salespeople will look in the same places. Develop the ability to seek out business using a creative and imaginative approach. Keep your eye on the daily newspapers and business magazines for any stories of companies getting export orders, expanding their premises, taking on new staff or introducing new products.

The information you gather will be useful in planning original opening statements. Note business people in the news, promotions and new appointments to senior management. If you specialize in sales to a particular market, dissect the monthly trade journals for any relevant information that may lead to orders. Get into the habit of doing this automatically, every day, not just when orders are getting thin on the ground.

Cold canvassing

Ten to 15 years ago, cold calling was the way to increase sales. This involved trekking from office to office for the purpose of gathering information, setting up an appointment and selling. Today, there is a tendency to make approaches by telephone, mail shot or letter. However, while cold calling never has been the most popular aspect of selling, it can yield profitable results. The amount of visual information available whenever you call to a customer's premises allows you to:

- see at first hand opportunities for your products
- observe the size of the organization
- see their products or services and how they do their selling
- talk to staff for the purpose of gleaning important information
- find out the name of your prospective contact.

The most important reason for using this method is that today only a tiny proportion of people actually canvass personally for business; therefore you will see opportunities that others will not!

Mail shots

Most mail shots end up in the rubbish bin without ever being read, so you have to do something different to encourage the prospect to at least see what it's about. The advantage of a mail shot is that it establishes contact with your prospect. The only possible way mail shots can be effective is if they are followed up with either a telephone call or visit. Instead of going to the time and expense of a major mail shot, do a trial run of about 20 letters first. Keep your message short and make sure it has lots of *you* appeal.

Any communication with a customer should be worded in the reader's interest. The reader is not interested in you or the size of your company, so starting a letter with: 'We are the largest suppliers of… ' may get a 'so what' response. However, starting your letter with: 'Your company is highly regarded… ' may be read with greater interest.

Follow them up and monitor the results to see if the exercise is worth repeating. Most salespeople use mail shots as a flag-waving exercise and to keep their name in front of the customers. Frequently the effort versus the response indicates that another approach is required.

Personalized mail shots

Typically, replies to mail shots range from 0.1 per cent to 5.0 per cent and while telephoning each person mailed can increase that figure, it tends not to be worth the effort.

The experience of one financial institution that I am working with was as follows. They sent out 20,000 mail shots and received 27 replies. This wasn't surprising because the letter was too long and badly worded. I worked with one of their branches and we improved their hit rate to about 65 per cent – and this is how we did it!

I asked managers and staff to select clients most likely to benefit from the offer; we selected 200 prospective investors; each of the ten salespeople working in the branch were given 20 clients; I took the original mailshot and cut it down from eight paragraphs to two; the salespeople were asked to provide basic personalized information about their clients.

We sent out the letters drawing reference to this personal information. This information was basic. A typical letter was introduced thus: 'I know that this is a busy time of the year for you personally, particularly with the new export contract. However, I have a special investment opportunity that I think may be of interest to you and I am anxious to discuss the details with you! In summary what it will mean to you is...

The essential aspect of this letter is that the writer indicates personal knowledge of the customer and his business, which will encourage people to read with greater interest.

The letters were all followed up by telephone call (a number had already responded). Of the 200 letters that went out, 123 sales resulted. This idea was so successful that the company immediately suspended mail shots from their marketing campaign and applied the new approach to all other branches.

A personal letter

This same idea applies also to generating new business. Instead of sending aimless mail shots ,write two or three personal letters per day to prospective customers seeking a meeting. I know of many salespeople who, by using this approach, have increased success rate over mail shots from 2 per cent to 70 per cent.

Exhibitions

These can be a tremendous source of leads and can keep you going for months. However, the floor space in a major exhibition can be enormously costly before you even put your stand up. What you can do is arrange a smaller exhibition, perhaps with two other non-competitive but related businesses. The other companies' customers may become your own.

Swapping leads

Salespeople don't do this in any sort of organized fashion,

but what is to stop you and your company forming an association with other, non-competitive companies to swap leads and prospects? You would be able to get all the relevant information you need about the prospect and so would be able to tailor the presentation, making it more pertinent to their needs. I formed a breakfast club made up of salespeople selling non-competitive products and we met every six weeks to exchange information – it was invaluable to all of us.

Your customers

This source is all too often overlooked. When we get a sale we are reluctant to push our luck by asking for referrals. Competition being what it is, when customers buy from you they do so for what they think is a very good reason. If you have a good relationship with happy customers, consider asking:

- for names of people who they feel may benefit from your product or service
- for other people in the company who might also be prospects
- if you can use their name as an introduction

How you ask is important. If you say: 'Can you think of anybody who… ?', the response will more than likely be: 'No, I can't think of anybody at the moment.' Question skilfully and make sure your customer is aware that you will use his name diplomatically and in a way that will not alter his relationship. Get more out of your present customers. Nothing surpasses customer satisfaction for new business leads.

Old customer records

Look through old records periodically. A prospect who didn't buy a year ago may be in the market for your products now or in the future. Perhaps the company has a new Sales Manager or Purchasing Officer with whom you could establish contact.

Telephone canvassing

This can be very effective because it's quick and relatively inexpensive. You can establish quickly whether your prospect warrants a personal call. While you may not talk to or meet your prospect during cold canvassing to ascertain potential, in conversation on the telephone you may be able to find out their present supplier and how much your prospect orders.

Customer records

Paperwork can be tedious and generally you should try to cut out as much of it as possible. However, one area of paperwork is essential: the formulation of some kind of effective system for recording prospect and customer details. By keeping those records up to date, you will be able to evaluate the status of a customer or prospect at any time.

It is a good idea to arrange your customers both alphabetically and geographically so that if you decide to visit a particular part of the city, you have a ready list of companies. Customers and prospects should not be kept together as they require different approaches.

Search for new business seven days a week. The very nature of our business is to be constantly aware of sales prospects. A social outing, a game of squash or a party are all opportunities to meet someone who may be a prospective buyer.

HOW TO MAXIMIZE YOUR PROSPECTS OF GETTING TO SEE BUYERS

I have seen salespeople pick up a telephone with as much enthusiasm as somebody going to the electric chair. They appear relieved when they are told that their contact is not available. These are all the symptoms of poor planning, organization and many failures. There are some fundamental points about using the telephone to make appointments:

- You must be able to offer your prospects something special.
- Secretaries who screen calls deal with countless salespeople every day; we have got to be a little more professional than the rest.
- The more information you give on the telephone, the less chance you have of getting the appointment.
- Don't allow yourself to get dispirited when not achieving your appointment target – even the world's greatest salespeople can't win them all!

SOME HELPFUL HINTS IN MAKING APPOINTMENTS BY TELEPHONE

There are definite pros and cons to making appointments to see prospects. With cold calling, salespeople can cover a large territory quite quickly but may yield a low number of live leads. Telephone appointments, on the other hand, must be carefully planned to avoid racing from one side of the city to the other.

- Avoid making fixed appointments unless you are certain to be on time. A number of customers will agree to an approximate appointment time, eg late morning or early afternoon.
- A very good discipline is to make at least two firm appointments per day – one first thing in the morning

and the other first thing in the afternoon. The rest of the day can be used for flexible appointments where a fixed time was not specified, or for cold canvassing.

- Set the objective of the call. Obviously you want to make an appointment at a suitable time for you, so what times and alternatives will you offer the prospect?
- Do you want to visit the prospect, invite him to your showrooms, or to an exhibition? Be absolutely clear about what you are trying to achieve. Anticipate his objections to seeing you and pre-plan your response and have your diary in front of you at all times.

Telephone appointments

Please note that no attempt is made here to offer a panacea for making sales appointments – it is an entirely personal choice. Add, alter, substitute or delete any statement until you find those that suit your selling style.

Unless you promise to offer something special, buyers will not see you. Unlike a physical call to the buyer's premises – where a meeting is already taking place – if you cannot inspire them on the telephone you may not get the opportunity to meet.

News approach

Most salespeople will get a pretty good opening statement from newspaper reports or television. For example, a news report may centre on: a customer's business; government grants; price increases; government legislation; new factories in the area.

An opening statement might go something like this: 'I was reading in the newspapers this morning that the government has granted £19 million to this area for development purposes. This will mean additional opportunities for our companies, and I would appreciate a few moments of your time to outline some mutually profitable idea.'

Referral approach

Quite a number of professional salespeople work only on recommendations from other customers. It is the most successful of all opening statements: 'Mr Shaw, I understand that we have a mutual friend in Peter Smith. He recommended that I should contact you as he believes I have something that will be of considerable interest to you.'

This approach can greatly increase your order intake by getting leads from customers who have bought from you. One word of caution: you should never use the referral approach from leads that have been passed on by people who did not buy. This would obviously weaken the presentation.

Bonus approach

The bonus approach is used by publishers when launching a new magazine: 'Free holiday competition', 'Buy this great new magazine now and get Part 2 free!' All these offers are 'carrots' to gain our interest. You can use a similar approach to encourage the customer to do business with you for the first time. Remember, every customer buys for a reason. Promises of genuine discounts may be all that are necessary to encourage him to make the decision to start stocking your products.

Customer benefit approach

From research, a cold call or information supplied by others, you may be certain that you can solve a specific customer problem, increase productivity or reduce costs. If that is the case, your prospective buyer will feel obliged to meet you; after all, that is what he is employed to do!

I recall a major buyer who would not take my calls but on cold canvassing, I discovered that my product could save him a lot of money. I telephoned his secretary who gave me the usual lie: 'He's in a meeting at the moment.' I responded with: 'Would you please tell him that I telephoned requesting a brief two-way discussion. I would like to show him how my company can save him over £60,000 in his annual printing costs.' Within ten minutes he was back on to me; we met, I got a major order and he saved his company a lot of money.

Arranging appointments with senior executives

It is obviously important to find an opening statement that suits your product, your customer and your personality. For example, if you sell to senior executives working to tight schedules, they may appreciate you getting straight down to business:

> 'Mr Customer, I know that you are very busy, so I will come straight to the point'
>
> 'I'm glad I caught you in, Mrs Troy, I have some ideas that I believe you will be interested in'
>
> 'I know you are a very busy man, Mr Smith;

however, I believe a couple of minutes of your time will prove worthwhile and profitable to you.'

Statements of this nature require considerable courage on the part of the salesperson and you can only use them if you really can prove that your buyer will benefit. You can expect buyers to say:

> 'I don't believe you'
>
> 'Oh yeah? Lets see you prove it!'
>
> 'How do you make that out?'
>
> 'The only people making money are yourselves.'

It is at this point that you need to have your story ready for the customer and do exactly what he suggests – 'prove it!' As you don't want to waste too much time on the telephone and the buyer is reluctant to give you an appointment, you can usually short circuit the dialogue with a firm final statement:

> I believe that my service can increase your productivity by 25 per cent and reduce your costs by a similar amount. I would like to meet you for about five minutes to confirm exactly what the savings will be on your present system. I have no way of knowing what your reaction will be but in any event I promise you that I will not waste your time.

If you have sufficient confidence in your product, your company and yourself, there is absolutely no reason why you cannot use any of these openers to meet more prospective buyers.

Service approach

Some salespeople prefer to telephone a company and introduce themselves in the hope of finding relevant information that they can use to encourage a meeting. An opening statement might be: 'Mr Bushe, the purpose of my call is to introduce myself and to see if there is any way that my company can be of service to you.'

This leaves it up to the customer to explain why he has not used your company in the past, and other valuable information may be gained by the salesperson. Finally, there is no doubt that the more opening statements a salesperson masters, the more likely it is that he will succeed in gaining an interview.

Remember, you are only trying to get an appointment

You are not trying to make a sale, so your objective should be to: gain the prospect's attention with a crisp, businesslike opening; get the prospect interested by explaining how your ideas can help him; close the appointment by offering alternatives. Or to put it in a nutshell: ring up, fix up, and hang up.

Tips for dealing with reception and secretaries

Decision-makers are busy people and it is not possible for them to see everyone who requests an appointment. While secretaries rarely influence the decision to buy, they can make it extremely difficult for you to speak to or see the decision-maker: it would be unwise not to recognize the importance of their role. Find out their names and treat them with respect; be pleasant and polite without being false or overpowering; regardless of their manner or attitude, never become rude or indignant.

When seeking their help in getting an appointment, use good human relations with phrases like:

'What is your opinion?'

'Can you use your influence?'

'I would like your help'.

When the receptionist answers, your attitude and voice should convey firmness but in a friendly manner. For example:

'Good morning, would you please tell your Managing Director, Peter Jones, that Gene Moore is on the line for him, thank you.'

There is an air of finality about this type of statement that does not invite further questions. In general, at this stage, one of four things will happen:

1. You will be put through directly to your contact, so be prepared.
2. You will be told he is not available. Just say: 'Thank you, I'll phone again'.
3. You will be put through to his secretary. In this case, you should repeat your introductory approach.
4. You will be asked the purpose of your call by either the receptionist or the secretary. When this happens explain yourself politely.

I strongly urge you not to deceive your contact with false promises of what you can do. Genuine interest-getting statements may inspire a secretary to put you through, such as:

'It is about a letter I sent him' (if indeed you have sent a letter)

'I believe I can save your company 25 per cent of your production costs' (if truly that is the case)

'I want her advice on a new idea'; 'She is expecting my call'

'I have some very exciting news for him.'

If you still fail to get through to your contact, do not waste everyone's time discussing the details of your proposal. Simply ask the secretary if he can make an appointment on your behalf. If this is not possible, avoid a lengthy discussion and explain that you will telephone back at a later date.

It is important to develop your own telephone approach, and great time and care should be devoted to it. While you may feel a little uncomfortable initially, after a few calls you will gain confidence and skill.

A standard introduction is a five-step process, for example:

'Good morning, Mr Smith'

'Thank you for taking my call'

'Do you have a few moments to talk to me?'

'My name is Gene Moore from Amalgamated Products'

'I am sure you are busy, so I will come straight to the point'.

One essential rule in making appointments by telephone is to offer alternative times when making the request. However, use your discretion, and avoid overpowering the telephonist. The purpose of asking the question is to gain control of the exchange.

When you have achieved your objective, confirm the appointment, thank the prospect for his time and politely terminate the call. Record the details of the conversation on your prospect card and enter the appointment into your diary. If you fail to get an appointment, it is essential to leave the door open for another call in the future. Your attitude on terminating the call must be professional and businesslike.

The steps to making appointments by telephone:

- customer greeting
- thank him for taking your call
- ask him for a few moments of his time
- introduce yourself and your company
- opening statement and purpose of your call
- listen to customer's comments
- ask for an appointment and offer alternative times
- be empathetic with customer's reluctance to meeting you
- close the interview.

How to maximize sales through proper use of the telephone

Few sales tools enable a salesperson to save or organize time with greater efficiency than the telephone, yet so many are inhibited by an innate fear of it – fear they will be unable to project their personality, that the customer will say 'no', or refuse to give them a hearing. Why should salespeople feel so intimidated by an instrument they have little difficulty in using throughout their social hours?

Taking a car into a city for the first time is a traumatic experience for anybody learning to drive, but having done it a few times without incident your confidence increases. This analogy also applies to selling by telephone: the more you do it, the better you become. Apart from selling by telephone, let us see how many other ways the telephone can help us.

- making: appointments; cold calls
- following up: quotations; mail shots; sales enquiries; a letter; leads; exhibitions and trade shows
- getting: repeat orders; referrals; market information; 'add-ons' to orders already received
- increasing: sales orders
- dealing with: low potential accounts; complaints; overdue accounts; service problems; customer queries.
- the telephone can also help you to: motivate inactive accounts; inform customers of impending price increases; check stock levels; maintain contact with buyers between visits.

TEN KEY POINTS TO GENERATING NEW BUSINESS

- If you don't have a constant supply of live leads, you can't grow your sales.
- Look for leads in places that other salespeople rarely consider.
- Cold canvassing – the least popular – but usually the most profitable.
- Set up a Breakfast Club for the purpose of swapping information and leads.
- Writing personal letters to new contacts can dramatically increase response.
- Ensure that all letters and mail shots have 'you appeal'.
- Do not try to 'sell' on the phone when making appointments.
- To get an appointment – you must offer something special.
- When making appointments, the objective is: ring up, fix up, hang up.
- Enlist the support of secretaries by using good human relations.

13

Forecasting Sales

Finally, we will look at those skills, which help us overcome the two major deficiencies that salespeople display most often:

- deciding what to do with their day, week or month
- identifying through simple analysis which of their activities require a new approach.

Planning is not just a matter of deciding what you have to do in the future, it is deciding what to do in order to have a future! By the end of this chapter you will: know where to focus your efforts for best return; know how to monitor your progress; and know how to set sales targets.

Before we discuss this chapter in more detail, please answer the following questions, if you can.

- How many mail shots do you have to send out to get a sale?
- How many telephone calls do you have to make to get a sales appointment?
- How many calls do you have to make to get a fact-finding interview?
- How many fact-finders do you have to complete to get to the proposal/quotation stage?
- How many proposals/quotations do you have to deliver to get a sale?

If you cannot answer these questions precisely, console yourself in the knowledge that most salespeople do, yet this information is critical to your development as a successful salesperson.

The law of averages works exactly the same in selling as it does in all other walks of life. For example: in my very first sales role I knew that I needed to make 16 telephone calls in order to meet six prospective new buyers to get three fact-finders which would result in one sale! This information allowed me to focus my efforts on where to make improvements.

IDENTIFYING SELLING STRENGTHS AND WEAKNESSES

An excellent way of improving selling productivity is to complete periodic activity analysis sheets. Good territory management and better time use will at best only increase the your efficiency and will not always be reflected in extra sales. On the other hand, when your activities are centred around identified effective selling tasks, selling productivity is ensured.

I have produced Day Planners (see Figure 13.1), Week Planners (see Figure 13.2), and Activity Analysis forms (see Figure 13.3) which can be easily reproduced on 3 inch x 5 inch cards. The feedback from salespeople who use them is consistent with my original objectives when designing them, which were to:

- encourage a disciplined approach to selling
- discipline salespeople to plan each day
- stress the need for daily sales targets
- provide a basis for 'actual' activity analysis
- identify selling areas requiring special attention
- establish new disciplines in sales-orientated self-development.

If you want to analyse your selling productivity you merely have to fill the cards in every day for one month and you have your own personal selling analysis.

SALES DAY PLANNER NAME DAY

CONTACTS NAME	PHONE NO	COMMENTS	TODAY'S TARGETS	NO
			TELEPHONE APPT	
			CUSTOMER SERVICE	
			CANVASS CALLS	
			SALES CALLS	
			PRESENTATIONS	
			SALES ORDERS	
			MAIL SHOTS	
			NEW LEADS	
			QUOTATIONS	

(a)

TIME	APPOINTMENTS AND MEETINGS
08.30	
09.00	
09.30	
10.00	
10.30	
11.00	
11.30	
12.00	
12.30	
LUNCH	
2.00	
2.30	
3.00	
3.30	
4.00	
4.30	
5.00	
5.30	
EVE	

(b)

Figure 13.1 *Day planner (a) Front (b) Back*

WEEKLY SALES PLANNER WEEK ENDING ________

TIME	MONDAY	TUESDAY	WEDNESDAY	THURSDAY	FRIDAY
a.m.					
p.m.					

(a)

SELLING ACTIVITY	ACHIEVED LAST WEEK	TARGET FOR THIS WEEK	IMPERATIVE TASKS	IMPORTANT NOT IMPERATIVE
Telephone Appts				
Customer Service				
Canvass Calls				
Sales Calls				
Presentations				
Sales Orders			NOTES-REMINDERS-FOLLOW UP	
Mail Shots				
New Leads				
Quotations				

(b)

Figure 13.2 *Weekly sales planner (a) Front (b) Back*

ACTIVITY ANALYSIS FOR PERIOD ____________________

TELEPHONE ACTIVITY	FIELD SELLING ACTIVITY	TIME MANAGEMENT
NUMBER OF CALLS MADE	TOTAL CALLS	TIME TRAVELLING
CUSTOMER SERVICE TYPE	CANVASSING	WAITING ON BUYERS
TOTAL CALLS FOR APPTS	CUSTOMER SERVICE	ADMINISTRATION
NUMBER APPTS GAINED	PRESENTATIONS	SALES MEETINGS
SUCCCESS RATE OF APPTS %	SALES ORDERS	MISCELLANEOUS
	SUCCESS RATE ON CALLS %	TOTAL MILES
MAIL SHOTS	QUOTATIONS	PRODUCTIVE SELLING
SENT OUT	DELIVERED	HOURS WORKED
RESPONSE	SOLD	NON PRODUCTIVE HRS
SUCCESS RATE %	SUCCESS RATE %	% TIME LOST

(a)

SELLING ACTIVITY SUCCESS RATES

TELEPHONE CALLS TO APPTS	%
CALLS TO SALES ORDERS	%
PRESENTATIONS TO SALES	%
MAIL SHOTS	%
QUOTATIONS	%
PRODUCTIVE SELLING TIME	%
MILES PER SALE	☐
AREAS FOR SPECIAL ATTENTION	☐
MAKING APPTS BY TELEPHONE	☐
CUSTOMER SERVICE CALLS	☐
CANVASSING FOR NEW BUSINESS	☐
SALES CALLS	☐
PRESENTATIONS	☐
SALES ORDERS	☐
MAIL SHOTS	☐
NEW LEADS	☐
QUOTATIONS	☐
TIME IN THE FIELD	☐
MILEAGE	☐

(b)

Figure 13.3 *Activity analysis card (a)Front (b) Back*

HOW TO MONITOR YOUR PROGRESS

Most salespeople are bad administrators and may look on these cards as extra paperwork, particularly when it is obvious that they do not replace a diary. However, my experience suggests that once salespeople get into the habit of using them, they find it difficult to operate without them. While most sales organizations have their own call and order analysis sheets, they tend to be ineffective because salespeople enter precisely what they believe the manager expects to read – which often bears little resemblance to what actually happened during the selling day.

Proper use of these cards will give accurate information on the following:

- success rate on telephone calls to appointments made
- success rate on visits made to sales gained
- number of presentations to gain an order
- success rate on quotations delivered to orders received
- total miles travelled to receive an order
- total time lost during the analysis period
- areas requiring special attention by the salesperson.

I give you my absolute assurance that if you carry out this analysis for just one month you will be amazed at the information it will provide.

The domino effect

It helps when developing your skills if you understand where your weaknesses are. A weakness in one area can create a domino effect right through your selling activities. If you are weak in making telephone appointments, your fact-finding visits are curtailed, which means fewer proposals and even fewer sales.

One of the best salespeople I ever trained accepted this idea in 1985 when he started selling. He uses the cards religiously and unlike most salespeople, he can tell me exactly what his hit rate is on telephone calls, fact-finders, presentations, proposals and mail shots – and he can produce records going back over the past 12 years.

The use of sales planners

Producing the cards is straightforward: hand write, copy them, or if you prefer, produce your own on a computer.

The headings under 'today's targets' can be tailored to suit your own organization. At the end of the week the information should be transferred to the 'Weekly Sales Planner'. After a period of four weeks, transfer the information to the 'Activity Analysis' cards. It is most useful (but certainly not essential) if a record is kept of business mileage start and finish over the corresponding period. Proper use of the time analysis charts mentioned earlier is also helpful.

There are other advantages to being well-planned and disciplined, it: let's you know where you are; where you are going; how you are going to get there; clears the mind; enables you to think and work better.

Carrying out such an analysis periodically will give your selling productivity a boost, provided you put the information to good use. Even the most successful salespeople should not consider themselves above the exercise: it is often the high fliers who have most to gain from sales analysis.

HOW TO SET SALES TARGETS

I truly believe that if you picked ten salespeople at random and gave them sales targets equivalent to 1 per cent of the sales potential of that particular territory – they would still only come in with 1 per cent. As a sales manager I can speak with considerable personal experience.

When salespeople are given a territory and its annual targets they usually make the cardinal mistake of looking at their 'patch' in terms of how they are personally going to achieve a specific sales target. In my opinion, this is the total opposite of what should happen – you should know (and sincerely believe in) what the territory is capable of yielding.

Setting all the 'agendas'

When you sit down to plan your annual sales campaign, this is also the time to set all of your year's objectives. What will influence your planning is:

- your company's objectives: long- and short-term goals; sales targets; new business development
- other departmental objectives: your customers' objectives; how often you should call; what they want you to do; how long you should spend on your visit
- your personal objectives: earnings; promotion; job satisfaction.

Not including all of these objectives in your plan does not automatically mean that you are doomed to failure. However, it is important to recognize the role they can play in keeping you focused and feeding your motivation to sell throughout the year.

If you were never told what your sales target should be

One of the most educational experiences in my career was in my second job as a salesperson. The company policy was that you were not expected to do any selling until you had completed your induction training. As I had two weeks to wait for my course my sales manager agreed to let me out in the field and get acquainted with my new territory. I was given no sales targets or training. In those two weeks I worked entirely on my own and opened up 17 new accounts.

When I attended my sales training I was amazed to discover that my colleagues from all over Europe had heard of my performance. They asked me questions about how I had achieved 17 new accounts in my first two weeks when the monthly target was set at ten. I worked in that company for a further three years and I never even came close to achieving what I achieved in those first two weeks.

This personal experience has influenced my thinking on the importance of not giving salespeople targets until after they have demonstrated what they can do without others imposing a ceiling.

Belief in your market!

Many salespeople make a difficult task impossible by writing off their territory before they have investigated its potential. If you begin by thinking negatively, you will uncover countless reasons as to why you will not achieve your sales targets.

One of the most morale-sapping problems for a sales manager is salespeople constantly bickering about territories and targets. If you want to endear yourself to your manager, start looking at your territory and targets from the perspective of how you will achieve – not on how you will not!

How to set targets

It is a most unusual sales team where everyone is on target at the end of the selling year, more often than not at least 30 per cent are struggling to make the quota. The purpose of this session is to ensure that you are not one of them.

One reason why salespeople find themselves under pressure in the last quarter of the year is because they have fallen so far behind that catching up has become a monumental task. Listed here are many of the contributing factors:

- Failure to set targets early enough. Management are often responsible, giving the sales team their budgets when the new year is already several weeks old!
- Wasting positive selling time convincing yourself that the targets are unachievable rather than getting down to serious planning.
- Robbing Peter to pay Paul. In an effort to achieve year

end results, normal prospecting is put on hold and all efforts go into 'closing' all outstanding proposals. This frequently results in us having no 'live' proposals to work with in the new selling year. It is further compounded by the fact that, as normal selling activity was suspended, your supply of appointments, fact-finders and proposals is much too low to meet your first months targets.

- Failure to set targets properly and monitor progress. We tend not to concern ourselves about targets until it is obvious that we have fallen behind. What started out as a target of one sale per day becomes 1.5 then 2.0 then 2.5 and this is undoubtedly, the biggest contributor to sales failure.
- Inability to plan for unforeseen circumstances. If you set out to achieve 100 per cent of target without allowing for many of the things that will inevitably go wrong, you will do well to achieve 90 per cent.

Putting the targets down on paper

Your previous selling trends are extremely helpful when setting personal targets because you are working on the basis of what 'actually' happened. Unless you do something very different there is every chance that your performance will closely mirror what you did in the past!

What is your average sale?

In setting targets be sure to work out your average sale. For example, if over a given period your total sales were £500,000 and you sold to 100 customers your average sale is £5,000. When carrying out this exercise be sure to exclude any freak one-off sales which may artificially increase your averages.

Apply Murphy's Law

As we know, anything that can go wrong will go wrong at the worst possible time. Plan your year on the basis of some things not going according to plan. A big order is cancelled, your car is off the road for major service and you lose your top customer. Taking all these factors into consideration, by how much do you think you should increase your targets to ensure that you achieve at least 100 per cent of budgeted sales? (in the Example B on page 237 I have applied an additional 5 per cent as a safety net – this is the minimum that a target should be inflated)

Work out the individual monthly targets!

A cardinal mistake made by salespeople is to take their annual target of say £1,200,000 and divide it by 12 to work out the monthly quota of £100,000 – this will inevitably cause problems. What is not taken into account is:

- some months have five weeks while others have four
- you will have public holidays in one month and not in others
- annual leave must impact monthly sales?
- what about scheduled days for training or sales meetings?

Because you know that these things are definitely going to happen, it is wise to build them into your annual planning. So instead of your year being broken into 12 equal targets as in Figure 13.4 example A, it more closely resembles example B.

Example B

January	10,000
February	10,000
March	10,000
April	10,000
May	10,000
June	10,000
July	10,000
August	10,000
September	10,000
October	10,000
November	10,000
December	10,000
Total	1.2m

This is a recipe for failure. There is no way that all months can be treated equally.

Example B

January	11,500
February	10,500
March	13,000
April	13,000
May	13,000
June	9,500
July	8,500
August	4,000
September	11,000
October	12,000
November	11,000
December	8,000
Total	1.25m

This example takes into account, annual leave and seasonal adjustments.

Figure 13.4

Calculate the actual number of days available to sell

The number of selling days available to you is obviously important because they have a serious influence on your daily targets. Use Figure 13.5 as a guide and work out the number of days that you can logically expect to be able to sell! If you expect to be in your office for two days every week that will obviously need to be listed.

To deduct from 365 days

Weekends	120 days
Annual leave	25 days
Public holidays	8 days
Monthly sales meetings 12 x half days	6 days
Projected days lost through illness	5 days
Days left to sell!	201 days

Figure 13.5

Number of calls to fact-finders

It may be tedious but it is worth every moment invested. Take out your diary and your sales reports or any other

> **Take any extended selling period, 12 months perferably but six or three months will do.**

> **Count up the number of visits made.**
> **Extract number of fact-finders completed**
> **Divide fact-finders into number of calls**
>
> **This will give you your hit rate on calls to fact-finders**
> **eg I need to make... calls to get one fact-finder.**

Figure 13.6

information that you have available. The longer the period of appraisal, the more secure the information. Ideally, if you have accurate statistics going back over 12 months the data is of greater value than if you were appraising a performance over three months – but if that is all you have to work on then so be it!

Whatever period you select to appraise your performance, use exactly the same period for the rest of your calculations on fact-finders and proposals! (See Figure 13.6.)

Number of fact-finders to a proposal

Apart from the fact that this information is invaluable to achieving targets, it also highlights the need for urgent action if the figures indicate a serious weakness in any element of your performance! (See Figure 13.7.)

This information not only assists hit rates it also indicates the quality of your calls

How many fact-finders completed?
How many resulted in a proposal?
Divide fact-finders into number of proposals
This will give you a hit rate.

eg I need to complete... fact-finders to submit one proposal.

Figure 13.7

Number of proposals to sales

The only information required in this crucial part of the exercise is the number of sales gained from proposals. Any outstanding proposals should not be included. (See Figure 13.8.)

Using the *exact same appraisal period* as you used to uncover your fact-finding rate.

How many proposals were sent out?
How many have resulted in a sale?
Divide successes into number of failures
This will tell you your hit rate.

eg I need to submit... proposals to get one sale

Figure 13.8

Information now available

Any salesperson that diligently accumulates this valuable data should have little difficulty in not only achieving targets but exceeding them. (See Figure 13.9.)

What we now know is...

How much we need to inflate the sales target
How to target each individual month
What we calculate to be the average sale
Number of calls to a fact-finder
Number of fact-finders to a proposal
Number of proposals to a sale

Let us see how this information can assist us in setting the annual target!

Figure 13.9

SETTING YOUR SALES TARGETS

By following these simple steps there is absolutely no reason why you can not, with some precision, predict what should happen throughout the coming selling year! Try to look on this discipline as your own personal sales management system – if you do, your sales manager will be happier and so will you! (See Figure 13.10.)

Annual Sales Target	1.000.000
Safety Net (add 5%)	50.000
Target to Be Achieved	1.050.000
Number of days to sell	201
Sales required to reach target	210
Sales required per day	2.01
Value of average sale	5,000
Calls to be made per day	8
Fact-finders to be completed	6
Proposals to be submitted	5
To sell 2 in 5 proposals @ 5000 per sale	10.000
210 sales @ 5000 per sale = 1.050.000	

Figure 13.10

Measuring and monitoring

It is important to monitor this system from day one, you have everything to gain and absolutely nothing to lose. If you go astray, you have an immediate monitoring system which, if corrective action is taken, will put you back on target immediately. It allows you to plan for equity of effort over the selling year and prevents serious pressures in the last few weeks – which directly affect motivation and your attitude going into the next selling campaign!

Finally, a few words of comfort!

I believe that any salesperson who applies these fundamentals to sales targets has an excellent chance of achieving budgeted sales consistently. However, by also applying the skills in this course you will also increase: the quality of the prospects that you visit; the quality of your own performance; significantly improve your fact-finding skills;

increase your hit rate on proposals, a combination which will dramatically increase your sales!

TEN KEY POINTS TO FORECASTING SALES

- Decide through analysis, which of your activities need a new approach.
- Planning is not something we do in the future – we do it to have a future.
- The law of average applies to selling – increased calls means increased sales.
- When effective selling tasks are identified – selling productivity is assured.
- Beware the 'domino effect' – one activity weakness can create others.
- Look on targets on how you will achieve – never on how you will not!
- If you were never given a sales target – would you perform better or worse?
- Work out how many days you have available to sell for the year.
- Keep a constant daily record of calls, fact-finders, and proposals and sales.
- Write up your annual sales targets and review against performance.

Index

Page reference in italics indicate figures